Also Available from Pronghorn Press:

Montana Spring, a Novel • Richard Magniet
Never Summer, Poems from Thin Air • Chris Ransick
Deep West, a Literary Tour of Wyoming

Anthologies from Pronghorn Press

Hard Ground 2000: Writing the Rockies
Hard Ground 2001: Writing the Rockies
Hard Ground III: Writing the Rockies
Dense Growth: Writing the Pacific Northwest
Dry Ground 2002: Writing the Desert Southwest
Foreign Ground: Travelers' Tales

HIGH COUNTRY
HERBS

High Altitude Growing,
Gifting & Cooking with Herbs

Cheryl Anderson Wright

www.pronghornpress.org

This book is dedicated to my Dad, who taught me to garden; my Grandma, who taught me to cook; my Mom, who taught me the joy of giving; my husband and friends, who offered endless encouragement; and to my three children, David, Mitch and Janie, and their families.

They are the reason for it all.

HIGH COUNTRY HERBS

Table of Contents

May Snow

Lilacs sag beneath their burden of blossom and snow
as a neighbor's sprinklers strew his lawn with crystalline jewels.
Bright grass peeks greenly from miniature drifts.
I hurry to brush the weight from delicate plants
put into the ground too early in my rush to spring.
Covered with a bright blue tarp,
I hope they will hold against the harshness
of the Rocky Mountain storm.

Every year I vow I will not plant before June,
and every year the false spring of this high country
lures me from the house with promises
of warm weather, clear skies.
In shorts and sandals, sweat streaming down my face,
stinging my eyes,
I dig holes, fertilize, water, visit every greenhouse
with dreams of English gardens so vivid in mind
I can impose them on my yard with little will.

Yet every year my tomatoes, basil, peppers, eggplant
and I fall victim to this deceitful country.
We belong in a warmer clime,
not to be beguiled, misled, betrayed
by warm breezes, soft scents, bright sunlight.

Cheryl Anderson Wright

HIGH COUNTRY HERBS

From a Tiny Seed

My dad was a gardener, so I began gardening almost as soon as I could walk. Not only did he garden, but he loved to experiment with new and different things. At a time when most people in our area grew only Dill, if they grew any herbs at all, we had Sage, Parsley, Thyme and Savory in our garden. He also planted vegetables that were unusual for our time and place, like eggplant and okra.

We lived in Iowa and gardening was easy. You planted it, you weeded it and it grew. Then I married and moved to Wyoming. Here I found that you planted it and either it didn't grow at all because of the soil, or if it grew, the wind killed it and if it survived the wind, an early or late frost did it in. Gardening in the West was a whole new experience and I found I had to start learning all over again.

I educated myself about composting and adding soil amendments; about how to protect plants from the frost and wind; about microclimates and zones; about alkaline soil versus acidic soil. I had to relearn things I thought I had known for years because in Wyoming you actually have to try to grow something. Nothing here is easy. Nothing "just grows."

In the years following my relocation to Wyoming I had

three children and when my oldest son began having debilitating headaches and doctors couldn't seem to help, I looked for reasons and a possible cure. I soon found that as long as he ate at home, where everything was homegrown and made from scratch, he had no problems. Whenever he would eat out, he started having headaches again. So I concluded that it had to be something in prepared food that was causing his problem.

Then my second son started having trouble with his joints. His joints, hands and feet would swell to the point where he couldn't even put on his shoes or his jeans. Again, this seemed to happen when he ate away from home. After a weekend binge on frozen pizza, hot dogs and barbequed potato chips shared with his friends, his hands and feet would swell so badly that I was afraid they might burst.

These experiences started me on the road to experimenting with herbs, trying to find a way to make things my children wanted, like barbequed chips, that wouldn't make them sick. They loved jerky, and couldn't eat the commercial version, so I tried combining different ingredients until I came up with a jerky that tasted good and caused no adverse reactions in my sons.

I soon discovered that my whole family liked my homemade seasonings much better than anything we could buy. Friends began asking for recipes. And over time each newly created recipe seemed to lead to a search for a better way to make something else.

About the time I felt I was really getting things figured out, a friend's granddaughter began having seizures. I asked about her diet. As I suspected, most of the meals she was eating were packaged prepared foods from the store, chock full of preservatives. I explained the problems my children had had and suggested that she try some of my recipes. Once all the child's food was cooked from scratch, the seizures stopped. She, too, was apparently having a violent allergic reaction to some kind of preservative.

Even though these examples might seem extreme, I think they are far more common than we might believe. And though the way I cook is much more time consuming, I think if you will try it, you'll find it worth the effort. Food cooked this way has delightful flavors and is truly good for you, as food was meant to be.

After finding so many people who were excited about my seasoning mixes, I began putting together gift baskets. I enjoyed making special gifts for my friends and in addition to my homemade seasonings I always included things like jams, relishes, and salsas. This led me to experiment with making giftable mixes for things like scones, breads, soups and spreads to add to my list of gifts from my kitchen.

Growing my own fresh herbs also induced me to try concocting herbal vinegars, flavored oils, salad dressings and a hot pepper sauce. I found ways to preserve supplies of grated garlic and ginger. I experimented with making many different kinds of pestos.

This combination of growing, cooking and gifting with herbs and all the wonderful food items they lend their flavors to holds a never-ending fascination for me. Many of the herbs I use in my recipes can be grown with success in the Rocky Mountain West. When I do have to purchase herbs or spices, I buy bulk whenever possible from a health food store. My goal is to cook ordinary food in an extraordinary way, a healthier way that results in great taste. I am always seeking and finding new things to make and new ways to make them and new friends with whom to share them.

Not all my efforts are successful, of course, but for me the best part of life is the learning.

And eating your mistakes can often be a real treat!

HIGH COUNTRY HERBS

Getting Started

"Okay," you say, "I agree with everything you said, but where do I start? I live in the Rockies and have soil that's so close to solid clay that I should be selling to a potter. If and when I do get something to grow, either the wind beats it to death or the deer eat it."

Soil

Let's look at your soil. The first thing you are going to need is a soil test. If you don't know how to go about doing this, call your county extension office. They will tell how to conduct the test. That test will tell you what you need to add to your soil. If it is mostly clay, or mostly sand you will have to add amendments. Even if it looks like fairly good loam, the pH may be too high or too low. The salinity of the soil may also be high. And if you don't know what kind of soil you have, you won't know what to add. The easiest solution and perfect starting point is a soil test, which costs about $15.00.

Many of you won't have access to leaves in your own yard, but maybe you can rake them up from the yard of a friend. You can also drive down the alleys in town and pick up the bags of leaves stacked by the dumpsters. Grass clippings are another thing you can use, but make sure the lawn they come from has not recently been treated with herbicides or pesticides as those clippings will kill your plants.

You will need manure. Whether you buy it in bags or get it from your neighbor's barn is up to you. Raw manure will have weed seeds in it, so old and rotted is preferred. You can also make compost bins and add alternate layers of plant matter and manure. Wet it down, keep it wet and in a few months you will have beautiful compost to add to your garden. Most gardening books have instructions for building and using compost bins and compost is a universally desirable medium, regardless of your garden's altitude and weather factors.

If your ground is especially dense, you may need to add sand. Your plants, whether you are growing flowers, vegetables or herbs, draw their nourishment from the soil. Just like you, "they are what they eat" and so you must start with a rich foundation of soil. While it takes time, it does make a huge difference to your garden's success. This whole process of upgrading your soil will take no less than one year, and may take several, depending on how much you need to add to make a good fast draining soil with lots of nutrients.

Another option you might consider is raised beds. Many garden and landscape design books offer lots of specifics for construction of raised beds as well as attractive options that will add to the overall design of your garden space. There are many advantages to raised beds not the least of which is having less far to bend over when you work in your garden! You can buy treated timbers from the lumberyard, or redwood or some of the new synthetic lumber which is designed for long life. One warning: Don't use creosoted timbers or used railroad ties as creosote is hard on plants, and can damage your hands and clothes.

If you are building your raised beds over existing lawn, you will also need ground cloth, which is available at your local nursery or garden store. This will keep the grass from eventually working its way up through your soil. Lay the cloth on the ground and build a frame from the timbers.

Place the frame on the ground cloth and start adding leaves, grass clippings, manure and kitchen scraps (not meat or meat products like bone, grease or fat). Then add your dirt, compost, peat or whatever else you can find until the bed is full. It would be good to do this in the fall so that by spring, the bed will be ready to plant.

If you are in a hurry, add bags of top soil, compost, manure and peat until the bed is filled and well mixed. Your extension office can give you a good formula to use for soil in the beds. Raised beds for herbs can be as little as four inches deep, but eight inches would be much better, and twelve inches deep would be better still. And you want to be sure to locate your herb garden in the sunniest spot that you have. In this country, with our short growing season, the more sun you can get on your garden, the better. This is a critical point that can make a great difference in your harvest.

What grows in this area and when do I put it out?

You can roughly figure that you can plant from seed after the 15th of May in most areas of the Rockies. A soil thermometer would be helpful, as you need the soil to be around 75 degrees Fahrenheit for best seed germination. I never set out plants from the greenhouse until after June 1, to be on the safe side. In Cody, Wyoming we are about one mile above sea level. We generally have the last frost of spring around the 15th of May and the first frost of fall sometime after the 15th of September, which gives us roughly a 90 day growing season. Anything more than that is a gift from above. I have seen it snow on the 4th of July in my time here. Whether that is the last frost or the first is subject to interpretation.

You will also want to know what planting zone you live in. Here in Cody, we are a zone 4. Most seed catalogues have zone maps and it is easy to figure out in which zone you live. This is very important to know. Each of our yards also has a microclimate, areas that are a little warmer or a little cooler depending on north/south orientation, shade and wind direction. This is more advanced gardening and there are many books available on the subject. For now, let's look at the zone map and use that as our guide.

What herbs will grow here?

Culinary Sage will grow here. This is not the "sage" (sagebrush) that grows out on the flats across much of the West. Sagebrush is an Artemisia and thus not edible while Culinary Sage is a perennial, which means it will come back year after year.

Some other perennials that grow well here are Tarragon, Chives, Oregano, Thyme, Lovage and many varieties of Mint, including Lemon Balm. Plants that must be grown as annuals in this area include Parsley, Rosemary, Cilantro, Dill, Marjoram and Basil.

You will probably want to purchase your perennials from a greenhouse. When buying plants remember, the variegated leafed varieties are pretty, but they are usually not winter hardy in zone 4. Be sure to check the zone before you buy perennials. If you have your own greenhouse or want to try to start them early in the house you can experiment but with the short growing season I have found the greenhouse varieties are a good bet.

I would suggest you start by buying at least:

2 Sage plants
1 Tarragon
1 Oregano
2 Thyme
1 Rosemary
2 Chives
2 Marjoram
1-2 Parsley
Savory and Lovage are usually hard to find.

If you decide to plant mint, it will be best in a bed by itself or on the edge of your lawn. Mints creep and will put out many rhizomes, or runners, that spread underground, put out new plants and quickly take over, so you want them in an area where they will be either easily controlled or where it doesn't matter if they run rampant, as they surely will.

I prefer to plant Basil, Dill, and Cilantro from seed. When your soil is warm enough, make shallow rows across your beds and drop in the seeds, then cover them lightly.

Plant the fern leaf type of Dill if you want the leaves for use and the Long Island Mammoth if you want the seeds. Plan to make several successive plantings of Cilantro as it bolts (goes to seed) quickly. The seeds of Cilantro are known as Coriander, and these can also be used in cooking.

You do not need exceedingly rich soil to grow herbs. Just make sure it is porous, that it drains quickly and contains organic matter (leaves, grass clippings, manure). You may need to do a perculation test. This will tell you how fast your soil drains. Here again the county extension office can be of help.

You should not need to fertilize your herbs, but if you feel you must, mix the fertilizer at half the strength the bottle or box recommends. Plant the herbs at the distances recommended on the packages and they should be fine. I like to run my rows from north to south, if possible, and plant the tallest things on the west side of the garden to allow the smaller plants some shade in the afternoons.

Herbs are relatively pest free. In fact, if you have insect pests or slugs in your garden, herbs will often act as a repellant. The herb most likely to be attacked by insects is Basil. If your Basil starts turning yellow and dying, aphids are probably the cause. You can try repotting it and spraying it with a pesticide, but it is very difficult to get rid of aphids once they are established on a plant. Deer also love Basil, so if you have deer in your area, you might want to fence your garden either with a high fence or one with a wire roof on it. Or you can grow your Basil in a pot and bring it in at night. This works very well for many people in Cody where the deer do wander through parts of town.

Rosemary is subject to powdery mildew. This looks the way it sounds. If the plant is covered with a gray powdery substance and is looking sick, it is probably powdery mildew. You will need to find a fungicide or else throw out the plant and start over. It will take several applications of the fungicide to rid the plant of this problem.

Now what?

Hopefully, now you have a beautiful robust herb garden. So what will you do with all the herbs? You can dry them, freeze them, make pestos and vinegars. But whatever you are going to make, the first thing you need to do is pick the leaves or stems, wash them and dry them. I like to use a salad spinner for this as it spins most of the moisture off the leaves. Remember, your herbs will have more flavor if they are picked in the cool of the morning. Heat tends to drive the essential oils, which give herbs their intense flavor, out of the leaves and back into the base of the plant, hence less flavor.

Herbs may be tied in bunches and air dried. Hang them in a dry area with air movement and little light. A basement or garage will usually work well as a drying area. You can also remove the leaves from the stems and dry them in a food dryer. If you are in a hurry, you can place the leaves between several layers of paper towel and dry them in your microwave. Do this in 20 to 30 second bursts and inspect the leaves between bursts. Be very careful doing this as you can catch the paper toweling on fire.

Certain herbs, like Chives, do not dry well. I like to chop the cleaned Chives by simply cutting them with a pair of scissors and putting them in a small jar and freezing them. Pestos, which can also be frozen, are a simple and tasty way of preserving and enjoying your herb harvest.

I will discuss the individual treatment of herbs further in the herb chapters as well as in the recipe segments of the book. One word of caution; when you begin cooking with herbs always use less than the recipe calls for. You can taste it and then, if need be, you can add more. But once the herb has been added, you can't take it out. So try a little, taste it, give it some time to develop its full flavor, then taste it again before adding more.

HIGH COUNTRY HERBS

Tools & Supplies

You will need a few basic pieces of equipment to work with your herbs, once you are ready to harvest. A pair of good scissors is invaluable for trimming plants and chopping the leaves for use. You will need measuring spoons and cups. A large colander or a salad spinner is necessary for washing the plant materials. I prefer a salad spinner because I am usually in a hurry and the herbs dry faster with this device.

A mortar and pestle are good to have, as well as a mini food processor. An electric coffee or herb grinder that you use only for herbs and spices is a wise investment. (Believe me, if your mate grinds coffee beans in the same grinder you have used for your chili peppers, words like divorce may be bandied about!)

A food processor or blender and food dryer are items you might want to consider buying, if you don't already have them. A small funnel is nice for filling jars. You might also want some kind of rack for drying, such as a clothes drying rack. You can also use coat hangers by tying two bundles of herbs together with about a foot of string, and placing them over the hanger. Then you can hang it from the rafters of your garage or the floor joists of your basement.

Of course, you will need a supply of suitable containers in which to store your herbs and to use for gifting. I am always on the lookout for small, fancy jars and bottles, tins, baskets, empty spice racks or vinegar and oil sets; anything that will make a pretty presentation in my gift baskets. After Christmas sales, garage sales and import shops are good sources of materials at reasonable prices. Involve your friends and family and you will soon have a ready supply of these items.

And as an additional note: I have to say that I have found that a sprayer to use with olive oil in the kitchen has been a boon to my cooking and eliminated the need for using commercial non-stick cooking sprays. It is a pump up device you can use both to prepare pans but also on your food. Mix olive oil and herbed vinegar and use it to spary on your salad dressing which will give you good "coverage" and cut down the amount of dressing you actually use. These are readily available from cook's specialty stores and in teh kitchen section of department stores.

The Herbs

HIGH COUNTRY HERBS

Basil

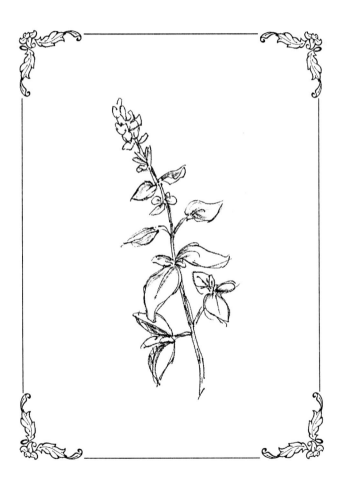

HIGH COUNTRY HERBS

Basil

Basil is a native of Africa and Asia, where it's highly regarded. The East Indians chose this herb upon which to swear their oaths in court. Basil is said to have been found growing around Christ's tomb after the resurrection, so some Greek Orthodox churches use it to prepare holy water and pots of Basil are set below church altars in Haiti. Basil belongs to the pagan love goddess Erzulie, and is considered to be a powerful protector. In rural Mexico, Basil is sometimes carried in pockets to magnetize money and to return a lover's roving eye.

Basil is one of my favorite herbs. It is grown as an annual here in the Rocky Mountains, which means it must be planted every year. I generally plant at least two rows of seed in late May or early June. There are many types of Basil and although my main crop is Sweet Basil, I do mix in other varieties because each adds its own essence to to the dishes in which I use them.

Basil tends to be a natural insect repellant, but aphids love Basil, especially in a greenhouse or sitting on a sunny windowsill in the kitchen. Aphids cling to the underside of the leaves and are very small, white, gray, green or black critters that suck all the juices from the plant and kill it. When I see them, I first try washing the leaves with soapy water, but I usually end up spraying the plants with a natural pesticide that contains rotenone or pyrethrin. Very often it is necessary to simply throw out the plant, wash and sterilize the pot (soak it in a gallon bucket of water in which you have put 1/2 cup chlorine bleach) and start all over again.

Basil tends to seed early so you will want to take several cuttings to keep it from seeding. As with all herbs, you want to pick it early in the morning before the heat of the sun drives the natural oils back into the roots of the plant.

Remember that the main focus of any annual is to make seed. The main focus of any gardener is to keep the plant producing and once it makes its seed it will start to die. So when the Basil begins to flower, you want to get busy harvesting. Cutting back the plants and removing the flowers will prevent the plant from producing seeds, therefore prolonging your harvest period.

I go down the row with a pair of scissors and cut it back to about four to five inches in height. By doing this I generally get from three to five cuttings a season. If you have only a few plants, you can pick individual leaves and then trim the plant stems back to encourage bushing.

I always dry at least two cups full of Basil. I strip the leaves from the plant and wash them carefully. Then I put them in a salad spinner to remove most of the moisture. If you don't have a salad spinner, you can drain them in a colander and then spread the leaves on a paper towel to dry. After all the water is removed, you can lay the leaves on a cookie sheet covered with fresh paper towel and let the Basil air dry.

Or you can dry the leaves in a food dryer or in the oven. In a gas oven, the pilot light is usually enough heat to dry the leaves. In an electric oven, you preheat to 200 degrees then turn the oven off and set the tray of leaves inside and leave them until dry.

You can also dry herbs in the microwave. To do this you

place the clean leaves between layers of paper towels. Set the microwave to half power and dry the herbs with 30 second bursts. Be very careful that you do not set the paper towel on fire. Check the herbs between bursts. Usually a minute to a minute and a half is sufficient to dry most herbs.

I make my main crop of Basil into pesto, which I then freeze in ice cube trays. Pesto must be made with fresh leaves, not dried ones.

Basil Pesto

Place about 1/4 cup of lemon juice in a blender, preferably freshly squeezed lemon juice with the seeds removed.

Add 2 tablespoons of a good olive oil

Now add 3 or 4 cloves of peeled garlic and purée

Slowly add the washed Basil leaves. It will take about 1 1/2 cup of leaves. Now here is where you can get creative. You can add spinach leaves, or Parsley or throw in a little Oregano. Each combination will have a slightly different taste. If this is your first experience with pesto, you might want to try about half spinach to give it a milder flavor.

Once the leaves are thoroughly puréed into a paste, you can add about 1/4 cup of grated Parmesan cheese and 1/4 cup of toasted pine nuts. Or you may use walnuts, almonds or hazelnuts for a different taste and a less expensive option. Any kind of nuts that you like will work.

Lightly toasted nuts work best as toasting brings out the oils, thereby augmenting the flavor. To toast the nuts, spray a skillet lightly with Pam or coat it lightly with olive oil. Add the nuts and cook and stir over a medium heat until the nuts are lightly browned but keep an eye on them as they toast quite suddenly.

As I said, I pour the pesto into ice cube trays and freeze it. Then I remove it from the trays and place it in large freezer bags to keep. One cube is about two tablespoons of pesto, or enough for an individual serving of pasta, or to flavor a vegetable dip or a salad dressing.

Often I don't add the nuts or the cheese until I am actually going to use it. If I am using the pesto to flavor soup or tomato sauce for pasta, I probably will not add the nuts or cheese at all. If I am using the pesto as the sauce for pasta or pizza, I grind the nuts in a small food processor and stir the ground nuts and grated cheese into the pesto at the time of use.

I use Basil in many dishes and in many of my herb mixes. You will find more recipes that use Basil, either fresh, dried or frozen as pesto in the recipe sections of the book.

Bay

HIGH COUNTRY HERBS

Bay

Many of the herbs that we use today have been used by mankind for centuries. The Bay tree, for example, was sacred to Apollo, the Greek god of prophecy, poetry and healing. The roof of Apollo's temple at Delphi was said to have been made entirely of Bay leaves, for protection against disease, witchcraft and lightning. Crowns made of Bay leaves became the mark of excellence for poets and athletes.

To Romans, Bay was considered the symbol of wisdom and glory. The Latin name of Bay is Laurus Noblis, with laurus meaning laurel and nobilis meaning renowned. Laureate means "crowned with laurels," hence poet laureate and baccalaureate. Bay was dedicated to Apollo's son, Aesculapius, the Greek god of medicine, and was thought to fight disease, especially plague, for many centuries.

In this area, Bay trees are grown in pots which are brought inside in winter. Their natural habitat is the Mediterranean, where they are perennials, often growing to a height of sixty feet. In a pot, with ideal growing conditions they may reach six feet in height. They are not too difficult to grow. They like a good bright light when indoors. An east window is fine, if you don't have a southern exposure. They do require a fast draining soil, as do most herbs, they don't like "wet feet," but at the same time they need to be kept moist. Misting is not a must, but a good misting or bath once a week or so seems to keep my Bay tree very happy. I also keep my Bay tree near my fish tank, which seems to please it.

I have never been able to find Bay seeds, but I have read that the plants may be grown from seed. Most likely, you will have to buy a Bay tree at a greenhouse or from a mail order catalogue. They are fairly expensive, as compared to other herbs, but with care a plant will last for years.

If you don't want to grow your own Bay tree, or your plant is too small to use the leaves, dried leaves are very easy to find in any grocery or herbal supply outlet.

Placing a Bay leaf in the bottom of a container in which you are storing a grain product, such as pasta, cornmeal, oatmeal, flour, barley or rice, will prevent weevils. You may also place the leaves under the shelf liners in your cupboards to keep out ants and other pests.

Bay leaves are used to flavor pasta sauces and in soups and stews. I also use it in my fish seasoning. You will find the recipe in the Seasonings section of this book.

Borage

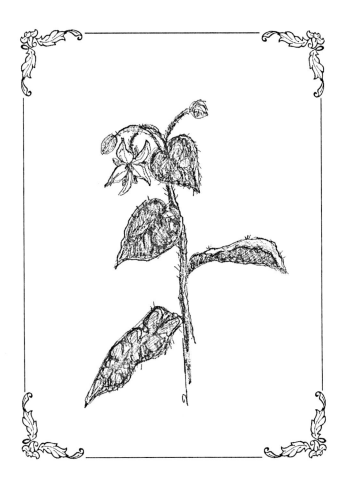

HIGH COUNTRY HERBS

Borage

Historically Borage is said to make men and women glad and merry, to comfort the heart, to dispel melancholy and give courage. The beauty of the plant should be enough to accomplish all this and more. The flower images have often been included in page borders of herbals and Books of Hours, as well as being embroidered on fine medieval tapestries and on scarves given to tournament jousters.

This plant grows easily from seed. It also freely reseeds itself. If you do not want it to reseed, you must dead head it religiously. This means to remove all the flowers before they have a chance to seed. But if unwanted plants do appear in your garden next year you can easily remove them or transplant them to another place where you would like them to grow.

Borage is a beautiful plant for your garden, even if you never harvest any of it. The leaves are large, silvery and fuzzy; the flowers are small and blue. The lovely little flowers are your goal for harvest of this plant. They taste like cucumber and may be used in salads to add a touch of color and a little surprise. Be sure to remove the small fuzzy leaves at the base of the flower before putting it into your salad.

You can also harvest the flowers and add them to white wine vinegar for a lovely blue color as well as a mild cucumber taste.

HIGH COUNTRY HERBS

Chamomile

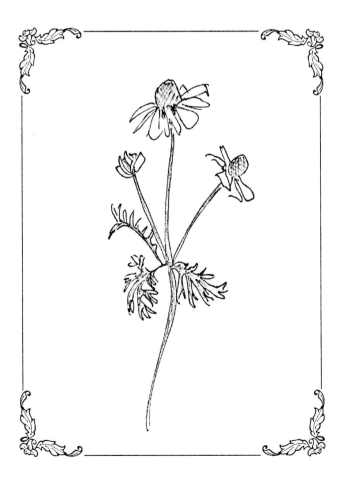

HIGH COUNTRY HERBS

Chamomile

There are two types of Chamomile. The upright variety is German Chamomile and it is this variety which is used for tea. It is the same variety used to make tea for Peter Rabbit after one of his close calls in Mr. McGregor's garden.

The more common variety that we find in greenhouses, at least in this area, is Roman Chamomile, which is a ground cover. The grounds of Buckingham Palace are planted with Roman Chamomile to withstand the heavy foot traffic. These two plants are not related botanically.

Chamomile may be grown from seed, although it is hard to find. German Chamomile is an annual and in some areas it will readily reseed itself. You may use the flowers from the plant either fresh or dried for Chamomile tea.

HIGH COUNTRY HERBS

Chervil

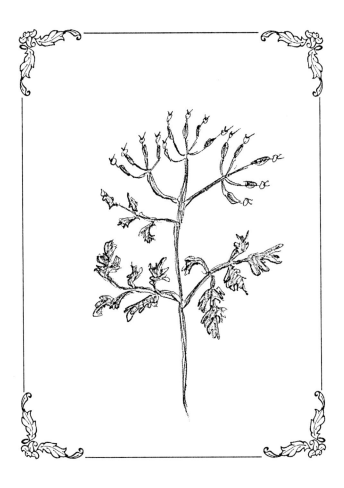

Chervil

This easily grown herb was overlooked in the past but is now increasing in popularity. Chervil has green fern-like leaves and a delicate parsley-like flavor, with a hint of myrrh. It contains vitamin C, carotene and some minerals.

One of the traditional fines herbes, Chervil is indispensable in French cuisine. It is very easily grown from seed and reseeds freely. Any plants that come up the following season are simply removed if you don't want them. You may want to make several successive plantings each season to insure a continuous supply.

This delicate herb does not dry well as the flavor is too delicate to hold, so you will mainly use it in summer when the leaves are fresh and green. It adds a nice taste to a summer salad. When you use Chervil in cooking, add it just before serving the dish, as cooking causes it to lose its subtle flavor.

HIGH COUNTRY HERBS

Chili Peppers

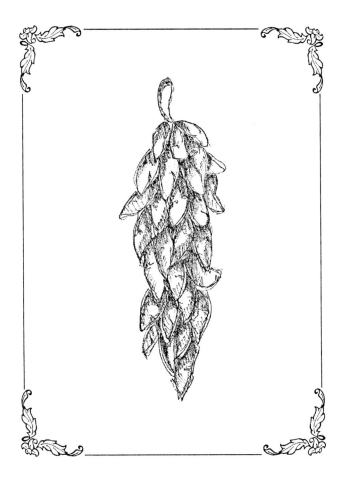

HIGH COUNTRY HERBS

Chili Peppers

Hot Peppers have been used in the tropical areas of South and Central America and Africa for somewhere in the neighborhood of 10,000 years. The earliest mention of Cayenne Pepper was in 1493, in papers from the voyage of Christopher Columbus. One of his men, de Cuneo, wrote about the Native Americans eating a Pepper-like fruit, like we eat apples. The native people called this fruit aji, but as Columbus believed it to be a variety of Black Pepper, he called it a Pepper. With the booming spice and herb trade taking precedence, the discovery of this hot spice was very important. Its use spread so quickly, and became such a substantial part of Indian and some Chinese cultures, that for a long while the Pepper was believed to have come from India or Indochina.

Peppers are one of the few spices we can grow well in our Northern latitudes. They do grow easily here and you can end the season with several strings of dried Chilies to use in making Chili powder as well as a few bottles of Hot Pepper Sauce, which my sons swear is better than anything on the market today.

No garden is complete without a selection of Hot Peppers. Again, I like to grow a variety of Peppers including Cayenne, Anaheim, Jalapeno, and sometimes Habenero. I dry most of them by stringing them on dental floss or fish line and hanging them to let them air dry. Jalapenos are the exception. I either can or freeze Jalapenos. I like to have several bags of them chopped for use in Chili Con Carne or Green Chili stew in the cold winter months.

Paprika Peppers can also be grown here. You pick the fruit when fully red, string them and allow them to dry. Then you remove the stems and grind the Peppers in your spice grinder for homemade Paprika.

You will find several recipes that use Hot Peppers in the seasoning and other recipe sections, but here is one for Hot Pepper sauce, the very Hot Pepper Sauce that my sons like so well.

Hot Pepper Sauce

A variety of Hot Peppers equaling about 1 quart.
You may use fresh or dried Peppers for the sauce.

3 to 3 1/2 cups vinegar

3 cloves garlic

1 1/2 tsp. salt

1 Tbs. sugar

2 Tbs. lemon juice

Remove stems from Chilies and put the them in a quart jar. Mix together the vinegar, garlic, salt, sugar and lemon juice. Pour it over the Chilies and let them marinate for 5 to 14 days. Put the Chilies and vinegar into a blender. Purée until well blended.

Pour this mix into a heavy saucepan and bring to a boil. Reduce heat to a simmer and cook until mixture thickens - about 1 hour.

Strain or sieve to remove seeds. Bottle as desired. Let flavors blend for 24 hours. Keep refrigerated.

Now I must admit, I only cooked this mixture once. The fumes burned my eyes and my lungs, the mixture burned my skin where it splashed on me when I was bottling it, and the pan I used made everything that was cooked in it too spicy to eat for several meals thereafter. Now I just keep adding the ingredients to the blender until I get to the desired consistency, then I bottle it. I don't cook it and I don't strain it. If you want a very pretty product you could strain it through a coffee filter, but I would only try cooking it again when I could have the doors open and a gas mask on hand. I would also use a pan that I never used for anything else. My sons seem to prefer the uncooked variety anyway.

HIGH COUNTRY HERBS

Chives

HIGH COUNTRY HERBS

Chives

Chives are an allium, a member of the onion family. The use of Chives was recorded 4,000 years ago in China. Marco Polo brought them to the West from China.

Chives are a perennial. They are very easy to grow in this area and are the first herb to appear in the spring, often bravely poking tender shoots up through the snow.

Many varieties are grown in China, where they are still used extensively in cooking. In this country we grow two varieties; the regular Chives and Garlic Chives, which are also called Chinese Chives. Chives are very easy to start from seed, or you can find plants at the greenhouse, or you might have a friend who will give you a start. They will grow in any average soil and in full sun to partial shade.

Chives grow in a clump and need to be divided about every two to three years. Once you get them started you will have plenty of plants to share with friends and family. I like to have about six clumps of Chives growing, four regular and two garlic.

Fresh Chives are wonderful chopped in salad or as a garnish for soup. I add them to salad dressings and sprinkle them on sliced tomatoes and cucumbers. You can use the flowers to flavor and color vinegars. People who like onions but have digestive problems will generally tolerate Chives very well, and they really appreciate an onion flavor that doesn't upset their stomach.

I wash Chives and cut them into small pieces with scissors and freeze them for storage. I have seen several references to drying Chives, but I have never found drying to make a very satisfactory product.

If you have a sunny windowsill, you may want to pot up some Chives and bring them in for use in the winter.

You will find that I use Chives throughout the recipes included in this book.

Cilantro

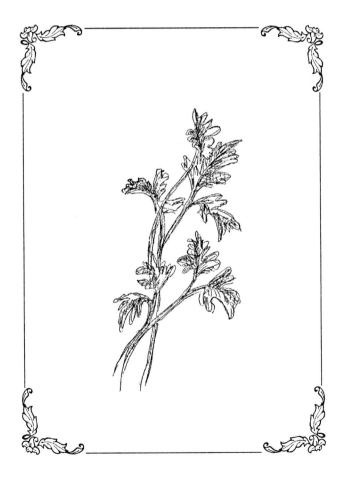

HIGH COUNTRY HERBS

Cilantro

Cilantro refers to the leaves of the plant. When the seeds are called for they are known as Coriander, which has been cultivated in Egypt for over 3,000 years. It is one of the herbs mentioned in the Bible, where it is compared to manna. Coriander was brought to Europe by the Romans, who mixed it with vinegar and Cumin to use as a preservative for meat. The Chinese believed it imparted immortality, and in the Middle Ages it was used in love potions as an aphrodisiac.

Cilantro is very easy to grow in our area and is a staple in Mexican and Chinese cooking. The Cilantro leaves are used in soups, salsas, curries and salads. The seeds are used in pickling both vegetables and meats. The seeds can also be ground and added to other spices for use in baking.

Cilantro bolts easily and will readily reseed itself, if you do not harvest the seeds. You will probably want to make several successive plantings each season to insure a good supply, as it does not dry well. But you can make it into pesto and freeze it to use in soups, salsas, vegetable dips and salad dressings. You make the pesto the same way you make Basil pesto, simply substituting Cilantro leaves for the Basil leaves. I always use only Cilantro leaves in the recipe, however, as the pure Cilantro taste is what I am after.

Here is a recipe for Cilantro dip for vegetables using Cilantro pesto:

Cilantro Dip
Makes

1/2 cup plain yogurt, mayonnaise, puréed cottage cheese, cream cheese or sour cream, or a mixture of 1/4 cup of any two of them. Mix together well and add one cube or two tablespoons of Cilantro pesto.

Now you may stir in 1/4 cup chopped, toasted pine nuts or walnuts, 1/4 cup diced tomato and/or red or green bell pepper, and 1/4 cup of Monterey Jack cheese. You may also add a few drops of red pepper sauce or about 1/2 teaspoon of dried red pepper flakes if you like a spicy mixture.

Be creative when you cook and experiment to see which flavors and textures you like best in this dip. This also can be thinned with a little milk and used as a salad dressing or it can be used as is to top a baked potato. Or add some to a taco instead of sour cream. Let your imagination go. And if you can't grow enough Cilantro to meet your needs, it is readily available fresh in most grocery stores.

Dill

HIGH COUNTRY HERBS

Dill

"Woe unto you, scribes and Pharisees, hypocrites! For ye pay tithe of Mint and Dill and Cumin, and have omitted the weightier matters of the law" (Matt.23:23). This biblical reference shows that even two thousand years ago herbs had such a high value they could be used to pay taxes. Now that you can have such a nice herb garden of your own, don't you wish the same held true today?

The chances are if you or your parents or grandparents had a garden, they raised Dill. This may have been the only herb they raised, the only herb you were familiar with as a child. The chances are also good that the seeds were used to flavor pickles and possibly cucumbers and onions with sour cream, especially if you came from a Scandinavian family.

Today it is common to raise both the old-fashioned Long Island Mammoth for seeds to use in making pickles and other dishes as well as a fern leaf variety for the leaves, which are used both fresh and dried.

Dill is one of the easiest herbs to grow from seed. And the Long Island Mammoth variety will reseed itself freely if you do not dead head it (remove all the seed heads) religiously.

After the seeds develop but before they get so dry they

begin to drop off the plant, you clip the seed heads and place them in a brown paper sack to finish drying. Then you can separate the seeds from the chaff and store them in a jar for future use. Or use the whole fresh seed heads in making Dill pickles.

The fern leaf variety is grown for the leaves, though it, too will go to seed. For the longest possible use, keep the plant clipped. Use the clippings fresh or dry them by laying them out on paper towels spread on a cookie sheet, or in a food dryer set on low. Dill also freezes well. Dill, of course, works well in salads and dips. You can also make a delicious mustard sauce to use with fish.

Fennel

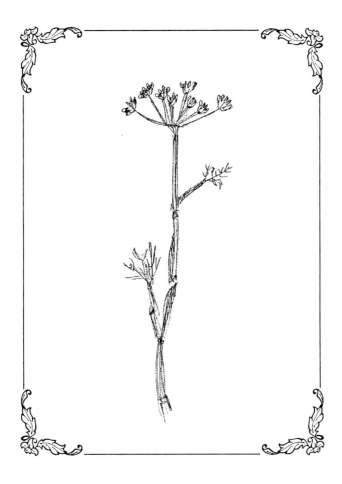

HIGH COUNTRY HERBS

Fennel

One of our oldest cultivated plants, Fennel was highly valued by the Romans and is still used in Italian cooking today.

"So gladiators fierce and rude
mingled it with their daily food.
And he who battled and subdued
a wreath of Fennel wore"

So wrote Henry Wadsworth Longfellow of Fennel. At banquets, Roman warriors took Fennel to keep in good health and Roman ladies ate it to prevent obesity. Wouldn't that be great if all you had to do was eat a serving of Fennel a day to remain slim and svelte?

Fennel is one of the nine herbs held sacred by the Anglo-Saxons for its power against evil and in 812 A.D.. Charlemagne declared that Fennel, with healing properties also to its credit, was essential in every imperial garden.

There are two main varieties of Fennel; the kind grown for seeds and the kind grown for the bulb. The Fennel grown for seeds comes in two varieties; either regular Fennel or Bronze Fennel. In Italy Fennel is a perennial, but here in the Rockies it is grown as an annual from seed. The seeds taste like anise or licorice. Some people also like to chop a little of the foliage into salads for an interesting flavor or as a garnish on soups.

As with Dill, you will want to wait until the seeds are fully developed, then remove the seed heads and place them in a paper bag to finish drying. Remove the chaff from the seeds and put the seeds in a bottle or zip lock bag for storage.

The kind of Fennel grown for the bulb is called Florence Fennel. This type of Fennel is grown in a row with plants eight to twelve inches apart. When the bulb begins to develop, you must hill it up with soil around the plants to form the large rounded bulbs prized in Italian cuisine.

Garlic

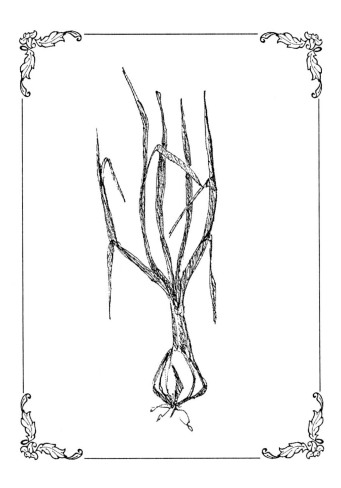

HIGH COUNTRY HERBS

Garlic

In ancient Egypt fifteen pounds of Garlic would buy a healthy young slave. Sometimes when the gardening gets hot and heavy I wish I could still buy a healthy young slave with my Garlic.

Garlic, in my opinion, is the prince of all herbs and neither garden nor kitchen is complete without a good supply of this glorious bulb.

You grow garlic from bulbs. Either find a variety of bulb that sounds good to you from a gardener's catalogue or find some locally grown Garlic. The Garlic at your grocery store is not the Garlic to grow in your garden.

Garlic comes in both softneck and hardneck with many varieties of each type. It is best when planted in September or October and allowed to winter over, but it can also be planted in spring as early as the ground can be worked. Separate each head into cloves and plant the individual cloves about six inches apart and about four inches deep. If you plant the hardneck variety of Garlic, a large hard serpentine stem will emerge in mid to late summer. Cut this off. Allow the plant to die back naturally and then dig the bulbs. When the tops of either variety are dry, it is time to harvest the bulbs.

I like to take several bulbs of Garlic, peel them and put them in the food processor with a little olive oil and some lemon juice or wine vinegar. I process them into a paste, which I put into a jar and store in the refrigerator. Then, I don't have to stop when I am cooking to peel and chop my garlic, as it is already done. I have kept Garlic this way for a year. If you have doubts about its freshness, or if you are making several jars, put it in the freezer.

I use Garlic in most of my recipes, so I like to have a supply of fresh Garlic at hand. Once you start using fresh Garlic, you will be hard-pressed to go back to using Garlic powder.

If you want to make your own Garlic powder, you can slice the cloves of peeled Garlic, dry them in your food dryer (you may want to do this outside on your patio) and powder them in your coffee grinder; the special one used only for herbs and spices, not the one your mate uses for their coffee beans. Garlic coffee would definitely lead to divorce court, if not murder!

Horseradish

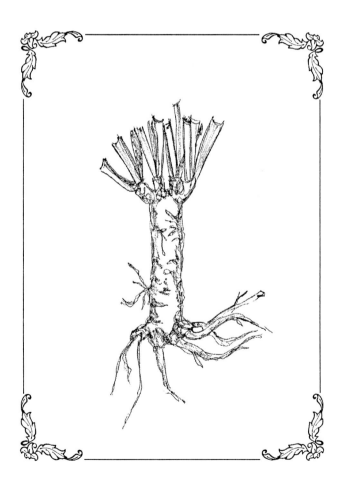

HIGH COUNTRY HERBS

Horseradish

Originally cultivated as a medicinal herb, Horseradish is now considered a flavoring herb. Germans and Danes began to use it in the 16th century as a sauce for fish. Around 1640 it spread to Britain, where it was used with roast beef.

This sharply pungent herb has been known to clear clogged sinuses in one breath. I can vividly remember helping my dad grind Horseradish when I was a child. We would be banned to the outdoors, where I washed the roots and my father turned the crank on the grinder. By the time the chore was finished, we would both have red swollen eyes from all the tears triggered by the volatile oil released by grinding and grating the root.

Horseradish is easy to grow. It is grown from a crown you purchase from a greenhouse or garden supply catalogue, or you might be lucky enough to get some from a friend. You plant it in rich soil and wait until the second season to begin harvesting it. An occasional dosing of manure tea or manure heaped around the plants does wonders for the flavor of Horseradish.

When I was a kid, we harvested the roots in September or October, keeping to the folk tradition of not digging the roots in months without an R. You may also dig the roots in March or April, weather permitting. Dig the roots from the ground and cut them away from the crown leaving about two to three inches of root with leaves. This is called the crown of the plant. Replant this portion into your Horseradish bed.

Next take your roots and scrub them thoroughly. You may choose to grind or, more easily, process them in your food processor. Add a little wine vinegar to cover and a teaspoon of salt and a tablespoon or so of sugar and store the Horseradish in a tightly covered jar in the refrigerator until you are ready to use it. Or you can store the roots in the refrigerator and grind them as you need, or you can store them in sand in a cool place that does not freeze. Another option is to wash the roots well, and slice them into rounds about 1/4 inch thick and dry them. Then you can grind the dried Horseradish into a powder to be used in many dishes. A bottle of Horseradish Powder also makes a great addition to a Meat, Poultry or Fish Flavoring gift basket.

You will want to use Horseradish fresh as cooking destroys the flavor.

Lavender

HIGH COUNTRY HERBS

Lavender

Izaak Walton is quoted as saying: "I long to be in a house where the sheets smell of lavender." I join him in this longing. The fresh clean scent of Lavender was a favorite additive to the bathwater of the Greeks and the Romans. In fact, its name derives from the Latin *lavare*, meaning "to wash." Long used medicinally, the herbalist Gerard prescribed it to bathe the temples of those with a "light migram or swimming of the braine". Today in many shops and health food stores you will find small Lavender pillows to be used for the same purpose.

The only variety of Lavender that will winter over in our Northern section of the Rockies is Munstead although in a sheltered micro-climate, Hidcote might survive. Of course, farther south in the Rockies other varieties are possible. You can grow Lavender from seed, although this is quite difficult as the germination of the seed is low, like Parsley and Rosemary. It also takes a long time to get a plant that will produce flowers. So you might want to purchase mature plants from a greenhouse or garden supply catalogue. Be sure to find a variety that will winter over in your climatic zone. Lavender likes a richer soil than many herbs so it will appreciate the addition of some compost or well rotted manure to its bed.

Lavender is used primarily for its flowers to scent potpourris. Or in packets of scents to place in drawers of linens and lingerie. I have also seen it included in Herbes de Provençe mixtures and some people enjoy adding some of the dried flowers to their tea.

Lovage

HIGH COUNTRY HERBS

Lovage

In ancient times the leaves of Lovage were laid in shoes to revive the weary traveler and at inns it was served in a popular cordial, which was flavored with tansy and a variety of yarrow known as Achillea ligustica.

Lovage is a large plant with a strong celery-like flavor. It is generally grown from a root division obtained from a friend or from a plant purchased at a greenhouse or garden supply center. It can be grown from seed but germination is poor and the seed is difficult to find.

Once the plant is established it may well grow several feet high and three or four feet wide, so give it plenty of room in your garden. It grows well in sun or partial shade.

You may harvest leaves for use in salads or soups throughout the growing season. It is often used to make a zero fat but highly flavorful vegetable stock for soups. The leaves may be dried and used in place of celery salt or seed.

The seeds of Lovage may also be harvested and dried for use in place of celery seed. The stems and leaves may be used in place of celery in soup, but use Lovage sparingly because it is very highly flavored and can easily overwhelm your dish. As I said at the beginning of this book, you can always add more, but once added you can't get it back out!

HIGH COUNTRY HERBS

Mints

HIGH COUNTRY HERBS

Mints

In Greek mythology, Pluto fell in love with a nymph named Menthe. When his jealous wife discovered what was going on, Pluto turned Menthe into a scented herb. The Pharisees collected tithes of Mint, Dill and Cumin. The Hebrews and later the Italians laid mint on the floors of their places of worship. Mint was long used to scent rooms and to freshen breath.

There are more than six hundred varieties of Mint. Many are used in teas and cooking. Some are used as insect repellants. Mint planted near your doorway will keep ants out of your house. Dried leaves sprinkled under the shelf papers in your cupboards will help deter insects.

Mints can be grown from seed. Many varieties are available from the greenhouse. Some are winter hardy in this area, some are not. I like to grow several varieties to use the leaves fresh and also dry them for tea. In addition, I use the fresh leaves to make Mint jelly and syrup.

I grow Lemon Balm as well and add it to ice tea in the summer, and to dried Mint mixes in the winter.

An ointment made from Lemon Balm called Herpaline is available at the health food store. This ointment will stop cold sores from breaking out if you apply it when you feel that first little tingle.

Mints are very invasive and need to be planted by themselves or in an area where they can be controlled by mowing, such as the edge of a lawn. They will grow well in full sun or partial shade and in any fast draining soil. And they smell so good!

Nasturtiums
&
Edible Flowers

HIGH COUNTRY HERBS

Nasturtiums & Edible Flowers

Nasturtium is a plant that is easy to grow from seed and has many uses in flower beds, herb gardens and vegetable gardens. The leaves and flowers, both of which are edible, have a peppery cress-like flavor, and add bite to salads and sandwiches. The green seeds can be pickled in vinegar and substituted for capers. Whole, the flowers make stunning garnish and add interest to soups and salads. The leaves are also high in vitamin C. And many gardeners plant Nasturtiums to help repel various insects.

Johnny-jump-ups, or Violas or Pansies, Violets, Marigolds and Calendulas are some of the other flowers that can be used in salads along with the previously mentioned Borage flowers. The flowers of Violets, Violas and Pansies are coated in egg white and then dipped in ultra fine sugar and dried for use in decorating cakes and cookies. Rose Petals are often used in this way also.

Rose hips can be dried and ground for tea or used fresh to make Rose hip jelly. Rose hips are very high in vitamin C. Rose petals can also be ground and rolled into beads to make a lovely scented necklace.

Calendula petals can be dried. They are covered with boiling water to make a tea, which is then used as a substitute for saffron in rice dishes.

You may use edible flowers and herbs to decorate a cheese

platter or wheel or a butter plate. Or to flavor and color a bottle of wine vinegar for a gift basket.

There are many uses for edible flowers in your cooking, but before you begin harvesting your flower garden for food it is essential that you become familiar with the flowers themselves, as well as which are safe and which are unsafe for human consumption. Flowers with which you are not totally familiar should never be consumed as some may be very toxic, causing severe illness if not death.

Oregano

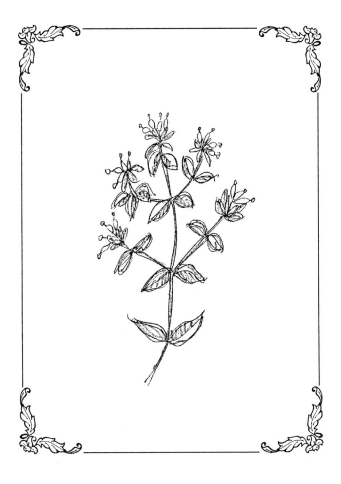

HIGH COUNTRY HERBS

Oregano

Oregano is wild Marjoram. The name comes from the Greek *oros ganos* which means "joy of the mountain." Can you imagine being in Greece where Oregano grows wild on the hillsides? Can you smell the scent of that sun warmed air? No wonder the Greeks believed Aphrodite created it as a symbol for happiness.

Bridal couples were crowned with garlands of Marjoram and plants were placed on tombs to bring peace to departed spirits. Aristotle reported he had seen a tortoise who swallowed a snake immediately eat Oregano to prevent death, so it was taken as an antidote to poisoning. Greeks used it to scent their massage oil and it was used in Egypt to heal, disinfect and preserve and was highly treasured.

A tea of Marjoram was advised by the herbalist, Gerard, for those who "are given to overmuch sighing." Leaves rubbed over heavy oak furniture and floors give a fragrant polish. And during thunderstorms, dairymaids would place Marjoram by pails of fresh milk in the belief that the plant would preserve the sweetness of the milk, as thunder was thought to cause milk to spoil.

Oregano is a perennial that is very easy to grow. The variety most often grown as Oregano is Origanum Vulgare or Greek Oregano. It can be grown from seed or you may obtain a plant from a friend, a greenhouse or a gardening center. Once established it is very hardy, even in our trying climate.

Oregano leaves can be dried for use in Italian and Greek cooking. They may be used fresh in salads and salad dressings, or to flavor vinegars.

Sweet Marjoram is a different plant. In this area it is raised as an annual, although in fact it is a tender perennial. Its scientific name is *origanum majorana*. It has a milder flavor than Greek Oregano, so if that one is too strong for your taste, you might want to try this milder cousin. This plant may also be raised from seed, or the plants may be purchased.

As with all herbs, full sun is best although the Oreganos will grow in partial shade.

Paprika

HIGH COUNTRY HERBS

Paprika

Paprika is a variety of Sweet Pepper. The seeds are a little hard to find, but several companies do carry them. I have never seen the plants available in any greenhouse in our area, but you may find them where you live.

You will want to start the plants when you start your Hot Pepper plants, either in your house in a sunny window, or in the greenhouse if you are lucky enough to have one. Plant the seeds in seedling trays ten to twelve weeks before the last frost. (Which in Cody would mean that you would start the plants about mid-February.)

A good place to start germinating your plants is on top of your refrigerator. Seeds don't need sun to germinate, but they do need heat, so the top of a frost free refrigerator is the perfect spot. When the plants break through the soil, move them to a sunny window or under some grow lights, or into a greenhouse.

When the weather is safe, somewhere around the first of June or so, depending on the year, set the plants out in a very sunny spot in well fertilized, fast draining soil.

When the peppers are red, pick them, wash them and string them on dental floss or fish line or other strong string and hang them to dry. To string the peppers, thread a long needle with your dental floss and run the needle through the stem or very top of each pepper. When your string is full, tie the ends of the string together and hang them in a dark, dry place until they are fully dry. Then break off the stems, place the peppers in your herb mill or coffee grinder and grind them into a fine powder. Store the powder in a jar or zip lock bag until you are ready to use it.

Parsley

HIGH COUNTRY HERBS

Parsley

Parsley was held in high esteem by the Greeks, who used it to crown visitors at Isthmian Games and to decorate tombs. Although the Greeks used Parsley medicinally, it appears that the Romans were the first to use it as food. They consumed it in large quantities and made garlands for banquet guests to discourage intoxication and to counter strong odors.

All Parsleys are rich in vitamins, minerals and chlorophyll, making the plants beneficial as well as attractive garnishing herb. So don't leave that piece of Parsley on your plate. Eat it. The least it will do is freshen your breath.

The two varieties of Parsley most familiar to us are the curly leaf variety, which is used in restaurants as garnish, and the flat leaf Italian variety, which looks very much like Cilantro and is the best Parsley to grow for cooking.

Parsley is difficult to start from seed, but it can be done. Plant the seed thickly in your starting pots, as germination is poor. Cover the pot with plastic wrap held secure by a rubber band. When you see the little green seedling, remove the wrap and set the pot in a sunny window.

Or you can buy your plants at the local nursery or garden center. Many years my Parsley winters over and comes back in the spring. If your Parsley comes back, remember it is a biennial, which means it will produce seed the second year. And remember, I told you the purpose of plants is to produce seed so they can reproduce themselves. So cut those seed clusters off as soon as you see them to keep your Parsley productive. I have had Parsley plants regrown for several seasons by following this practice.

Parsley has a delicate flavor. If you are using it fresh in a cooked dish, it is best if you add it at the very end so the flavor won't be lost. You can also use it fresh in salad and salad dressings.

Parsley is very easy to dry, and I always try to dry about a quart of it as I use it so much in my cooking. Several times during the season, I cut two or three bunches of leaves and wash them well. Then I tie my bundles together and hang them in the basement to air dry. When they are dried, I pull the leaves from the stems and put them in a jar for use during the winter.

Parsley may also be chopped and frozen, or added to basil pesto for a different flavor. However you choose to preserve it, be sure to harvest a good supply of this staple herb.

Rosemary

HIGH COUNTRY HERBS

Rosemary

Rosemary has been used by cooks and apothecaries from the earliest times. It had a reputation for strengthening memory and became a symbol of fidelity for lovers. Brides often wore garlands of Rosemary in their hair or carried stems in their bridal bouquets. And we all remember Ophelia handing her Hamlet a sprig and reminding him that "Rosemary is for Rememberance."

The Spanish revere Rosemary as the bush that sheltered the Virgin Mary on her flight to Egypt. As she spread her cloak over the herb, so the legend goes, the white flowers turned blue.

Medicinally Rosemary was burned in sick chambers to purify the air. During the Plague of 1665, it was carried in pouches to be sniffed when traveling through suspicious areas. In some Mediterranean villages, linen is spread over Rosemary to dry, so the sun will extract its moth-repellant aroma.

Rosemary is a perennial in the Mediterranean, where it can grow to more than six feet in height. Unfortunately for us, we must either grow it as an annual or bring it indoors in winter. Many people do not have good luck with growing Rosemary indoors.

I keep my Rosemary in a deep pot that has Styrofoam peanuts in the bottom for drainage, as Rosemary likes a light, well-drained soil. I use Miracle Grow planting mix and keep the plant in an east window, near a small fountain and my fish tank, which probably add much needed moisture to my dry indoor climate in this notoriously dry area. I keep the soil moist, as well, even though all the instructions I have read say to let the soil dry between waterings. Rosemary grows in climates that are humid, areas that receive a shower nearly every day in winter, so I take that as my clue to keeping Rosemary alive.

Rosemary is very susceptible to powdery mildew, so watch for this when you bring the plant in for the winter. (Powdery mildew looks exactly the way it sounds; it is a gray, powdery residue that slowly covers all the leaves, eventually causing the plant to die.) It is a good idea to spray the plant with an organic fungicide before bringing it in just to be on the safe side.

For culinary use, get your plant from a green house. Rosmarinus officinalis is probably the best plant to use for cooking and one of the easiest to find and to grow. Once you have a plant growing, you can snip fresh foliage from it year round as needed. The ones that are shaped like pine trees or topiaries and sold at big chain stores like Wal-mart at Christmas are generally too piney to be good for use in food.

Rosemary Potatoes

One of my favorite uses of Rosemary is with small red potatoes. Cut the potatoes in half, place them in a lightly oiled cake pan, cut sides down and spray them with olive oil. Sprinkle them with Rosemary and bake at 375 degrees for 30 to 45 minutes until they are cooked through and nicely browned on the bottom.

They are simply delicious. Add baked chicken and steamed asparagus and you have a meal fit for a king as well as for friends and family.

Sage

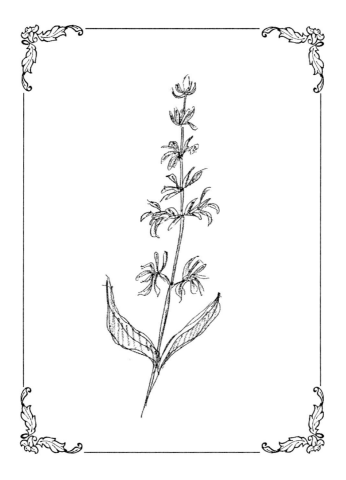

HIGH COUNTRY HERBS

Sage

"The desire of Sage is to render man immortal," instructs a late medieval treatise. Sage has been highly praised throughout history and on many continents for its powers of longevity. Sage was so valued by the Chinese in the 17th century that Dutch merchants found the Chinese would trade three chests of China tea for one of sage leaves

The name *salvia*, comes from the Latin *salvere*, which means "to be in good health, to cure, to save," reflects its benevolent reputation. To Romans, it was a sacred herb gathered with ceremony. The person appointed to gather the Sage would make sacrifices of bread and wine, wear a white tunic and approach the plant with clean bare feet.

We must not mistake culinary Sage with our native sagebrush, which is an artemisia and may be very bad for your health if consumed. A variety of artemisia called wormwood has been distilled to make an alcoholic beverage called Absinthe, which is illegal in the United States as it is very addictive and after long use causes blindness and eventually death.

Culinary Sage plants are usually purchased from a greenhouse, although it is possible to grow them from seed. One or possibly two plants are sufficient for your garden. Like most herbs, Sage will grow well in full sun or partial shade in an average, well-drained soil. Sage is a perennial in our zone and will grow very well for several years. You can divide large Sage plants and you also might want to try growing some from cuttings.

You will want to harvest the leaves of your Sage before the plant blooms. If you plan to dry a great deal of Sage, you may want to keep the plant pruned to prevent blossoming. As with all herbs, pick the leaves early in the morning while the oils are still present, wash thoroughly and dry as you do the other herbs. You can hang herbs in clumps to dry them, but they have a tendency in this area to become very dusty, so other methods are preferable. If you want the scent of drying Sage in your kitchen, by all means hang a few sprigs, but discard them if they get dusty.

Sage is used mainly with poultry and beans. You will find several recipes that call for Sage in other sections of this book.

Savory

Summer Savory

Winter Savory

HIGH COUNTRY HERBS

Savory

Virgil, in a poem of country life, described Savory as highly aromatic and valuable when planted near beehives. Romans added it to sauces and vinegars, which they used liberally. They also introduced it into northern Europe, where it became valued as a disinfectant. It was brought to North America by the earliest of settlers.

Savory is probably not familiar to most people. It comes in two varieties, Summer, which is an annual, and Winter, which is a perennial, although not always in our area of the Rockies. It is considered to be a zone 5 plant and most of the time we are definitely zone 4. With its peppery spiciness, it is one of the oldest flavoring herbs and has long been considered an antiseptic herb beneficial to the whole digestive tract. In appearance, it looks a great deal like Rosemary and until you are very familiar with herbs it will be hard for you to tell the difference.

The plants are very hard to come by in this area. I have rarely seen them in a greenhouse. The one I did find was not labeled and even the people who ran the greenhouse didn't know what it was. You can grow both Summer and Winter Savory from seed, though it is difficult to find. It's well worth the effort.

Traditionally Savory has been used to flavor bean dishes. I also use it in my Poultry Seasoning.

HIGH COUNTRY HERBS

Tarragon

HIGH COUNTRY HERBS

Tarragon

The name Tarragon is derived from a combination of the French estragon and Latin *dracunulus*, which mean "little dragon." The name may come from Tarragon's fiery tang, or from its serpent-like roots. "Dragon" herbs were once thought to cure the bite of venomous snakes. Tarragon was also chewed to sweeten the breath.

Tarragon cannot be grown from seed so you will either have to buy a plant or get a division from a friend. Tarragon, like most herbs, will do better in full sun. And like most herbs, it is not too particular about soil, as long as the ground is quick draining. Most herbs do not like "wet feet." However you obtain your plant, one plant is enough as Tarragon is a prolific grower. Before the end of the season you will have a good supply of Tarragon to dry or freeze or use to flavor wine vinegar. If you are fond of the taste of Tarragon, you can also make it into a pesto to be used with fish, pasta or in dips or salad dressings.

Tarragon is very easy to grow in our climate, often reaching a height of about three feet. The more you trim it, the better the plant likes it. To dry the leaves, wash them well, then strip them from the plant. Lay them out on a cookie sheet lined with paper towels and let them air dry or dry them in a food dryer set on the lowest temperature so as not to drive out the natural oils.

Tarragon couples well with fish. If you are lucky enough to have some fresh trout, lay a stem of Tarragon inside, in the center of a whole trout. Add a squeeze of fresh lemon juice, a sprinkle of lemon pepper and grill it until it is brown and crispy on the outside and tender and moist on the inside.

You may also want to place four or five stems in a bottle of wine vinegar with a clove or two of garlic for a delightfully flavored gift. Tarragon can also be made into a pesto and frozen to enjoy with pasta or as a fish sauce during the cold Rocky Mountain winters.

Thyme

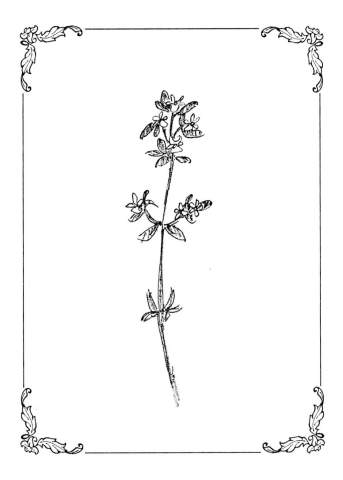

HIGH COUNTRY HERBS

Thyme

Thyme is another herb that we can trace back to the Greeks and Romans. To Greeks, it denoted graceful elegance: "to smell of Thyme" was an expression of stylish praise. After bathing, Greeks would include oil of Thyme in their massage. Thymus may derive from the Greek word *thymon*, meaning "courage."

Roman soldiers bathed in Thyme water to give themselves vigor. During the Middle Ages, European ladies embroidered a sprig of Thyme on tokens for their knights-errant. A soup recipe of 1663 recorded use of Thyme and beer to overcome shyness, while Scottish highlanders drank tea made of wild Thyme for strength and courage, and to prevent nightmares. A recipe from the 1600s guaranteed that one "would see fairies" after ingesting the concoction.

Thyme is a powerful antiseptic and its preservative properties were well known to Egyptians, who used it for embalming.

Thyme is one of the easiest to grow of all the herbs and also one of the hardiest. Thyme grows vigorously in full sun, and will also do well in partial shade. It is so hardy it can be used as a ground cover in the rows of your herb garden. Walking on it will not damage it and imparts Thyme's heady fragrance to your Rocky Mountain yard, making it smell like a sunny Mediterranean hillside.

Thyme is one of the most tedious of herbs to harvest as the leaves are so small, but the flavor they impart makes them worth the effort. You clip off handfuls of stems with your kitchen sheers and wash them thoroughly. Then dry them either in a salad spinner or by placing them in a colander. Then remove the leaves from the stems and lay them on a cookie sheet covered with paper towels and let them air dry or dry them in the oven, food dryer or microwave as described in the chapter on Basil.

Thyme is used in many dishes and seasoning mixes, which you will find throughout the recipe section, and you will need to have about two cups of dried Thyme on hand to see you through a year of cooking and gifting.

HIGH COUNTRY HERBS

Cooking with Herbs

HIGH COUNTRY HERBS

The Breads

HIGH COUNTRY HERBS

The Breads

Do you want to go to all the trouble of making soup from scratch and then serve it with some soft, air-filled, low nutrient white bread from the store? The smell of the soup is already filling the house, making your stomach rumble and your taste buds go wild. Give yourself and your family a treat by adding a good hearty loaf of homemade bread to the menu, for what is better on a cold winter day than warm bread fresh from the oven? And in this day of bread machines it is easier than ever to make your own breads. Of course, herbs only enhance the taste of this already wonderful treat. Some of the breads in the following recipes contain herbs and some are to eat with foods that have herbs in them.

And don't let some preconceived notion of the square loaves from a bread machine keep you from taking advantage of this wonderful tool. You can easily mix and raise the bread in the machine and then remove the dough and form it into more interesting loaves to be baked in your oven.

Remember, if you use white flour, use unbleached flour, as fewer of the nutrients have been processed out. The whole focus of cooking from scratch is making nutritious meals, free from preservatives and full of authentic flavor.

Most of these breads can also be used in gift baskets. Or

you can give it as a mix rather than a finished product by leaving out the liquid ingredients, substituting powdered milk or powder buttermilk where appropriate, cutting in the butter, or olive oil, and adding the herbs.   For instance, in the first recipe, you would put 1/4 cup dried milk and all the other dry ingredients in a bag, then add the butter and squeeze it into the flour. Just write out the full recipe and attach it to the bag, along with instructions to add the liquid ingredients to the mix, and you have a gift for one of your baskets.

These bread recipes are to get you started.   Once you begin enjoying the taste of herbs in homemade bread, you will happily begin experimenting with other combinations.

Herb Bread
Makes 1 Loaf

1/2 cup warm milk

1/2 cup warm water

1 Tbs. dried parsley

2 Tbs. sugar

1/2 tsp. dried tarragon

1/2 tsp. dill weed

1 Tbs. dried onion

2 cloves of garlic, crushed

1 Pkg. yeast

2 Tbs. butter

1 tsp. salt

1/2 cup sunflower seeds (optional)

2 1/2 to 2 3/4 cups unbleached flour

Combine water, milk, sugar, and yeast and allow to proof for 5 minutes. Add softened butter, onion, herbs, and salt. Add sunflower seeds if desired. Add half the flour and mix well. Add the rest of the flour until dough is easy to handle. Turn out on a floured surface and knead for about 15 minutes. Place in greased bowl, grease top, cover and let rise until double. Punch down and shape into a loaf. Place in greased loaf pan, cover, and let rise until double. Bake in a 375 degree oven for 25 to 30 minutes, or until top sounds hollow when tapped. Remove from oven, brush top with butter, remove from pan and cool on a wire rack. This bread makes the best grilled cheese sandwiches you have ever tasted.

If you have a bread machine, simply combine all the ingredients except sunflower seeds in the order listed. Add the sunflower seeds when your fruit and nut buzzer sounds just before the machine kneads the dough for the last time. Instead of letting the machine bake the bread, you can put it on the dough only cycle. Then if you happen to have a baking stone, you can shape the bread dough into a round loaf, let it rise and bake it on the stone. Or you can go ahead and bake it as above in a bread pan. Or let the machine bake it if you prefer. No matter which method you choose, the aroma of baking bread will fill the house with warmth, love and happy memories.

Focaccia
Makes 1 Loaf

Starter:

1 pkg. dry yeast

1/2 tsp. sugar

2/3 cup warm water

1/2 cup flour

Dough:

1 1/3 cups warm water

3 cups flour

1 cup whole wheat flour **or** semolina

2 Tbs. olive oil

1/2 tsp. salt

Mix starter and let sit for 15 minutes until foamy. Stir in rest of ingredients and knead for 10 minutes. Allow dough to rise twice, punching down after each rising. Oil 2 baking sheets and divide dough in half. Press each piece of dough into an approximately 12 inch circle. Brush top with crushed garlic and olive oil. Sprinkle with Parmesan cheese or Asiago cheese, if desired. Add a sprinkle of Rosemary or Italian Seasoning. Allow to rise until double. Bake at 375 degrees for about 20 minutes.

You may also use this dough to make pizza. The bread makes very good sandwiches and pairs well with spaghetti. You can also mix this dough in your bread machine and then bake it as described above.

Cheddar Chive Bread
Makes 1 Loaf or 3 Baguettes

1 1/2 cups water

4 1/4 cups flour

3/4 cup shredded Cheddar cheese

1/4 cup chopped fresh **or** frozen chives

2 Tbs. sugar

1 tsp. salt

1 3/4 tsp. yeast

Put all ingredients in your bread machine in the order given. Select the proper setting for either making dough or making the complete loaf of bread. If you choose to bake it in the oven, follow the instructions for Herb Bread.

You can bake this into a round loaf or into three baguettes. To make baguettes, divide the dough into three parts. Roll each piece into a long thin rope. Lay them on a greased cookie sheet. Cover and allow to rise until double. Bake at 350 degrees for 15 to 20 minutes, until the bread sounds hollow when tapped.

HIGH COUNTRY HERBS

Roasted Red Pepper Bread
or
Dried Tomato Bread
Makes 1 Loaf

1 cup of water

1/2 cup roasted red bell peppers, chopped
or
1/4 cup chopped dried tomatoes, soaked in boiling
water and drained

1 Tbs. butter

2 cloves of garlic, crushed

4 cups flour

1/2 cup Asiago, Parmesan or Romano cheese, grated

2 Tbs. sugar

2 tsp. salt

1 1/2 Tbs. chopped fresh basil leaves **or** 2 tsp. dried
basil leaves

1 Tbs. chopped fresh parsley or 1 tsp. dried parsley

1 3/4 tsp. yeast

Put all ingredients in your bread machine in the order given. Set the control for either baking the bread or making dough. This dough can be made into baguettes or a round loaf, as described in the Cheddar Chive Bread recipe.

A baguette of this bread with a jar of homemade soup and a piece of good cheese makes a very nice gift basket.

Indian Fry Bread
Makes 8 Breads

2 cups flour

1/4 cup powdered milk

2 tsp. baking powder

1 tsp. salt

1 Tbs. cooking oil

3/4 cup water

Mix all together, separate the dough into 8 small balls and roll out into 6 inch circles about 1/4 inch thick. Fry in hot oil or on a griddle. To make Indian tacos, top with chili, refried beans, cheese, lettuce, onions, tomatoes, black olives and salsa in any combination you like. Or drizzle some honey over it and enjoy. This is the fry bread that you get at Indian fairs and powwows.

Include this as a mix in your Mexican basket. To make a mix, mix everything together except the water and put it in a zip lock bag. Be sure to include the recipe.

Cheese Biscuits
Makes 8-12

2 cups flour (1 may be whole wheat if you like)

3 tsp. baking powder

1/2 cup shredded cheese

1/4 tsp. **each** dried marjoram, parsley, chives, and thyme

1 Tbs. dried onion, minced

1 clove garlic, minced

5 Tbs. soft butter

1/2 cup milk

    Mix flours, herbs, baking powder, and cheese into a bowl. Add butter and cut in until mixture is like coarse crumbs. Stir in milk and mix until mixture clings together. Do not mix too long or you will have tough biscuits. Form into a ball and knead gently 5 or 6 times. Roll out to 1/2 inch thickness and cut with a biscuit cutter. Place on a cookie sheet and bake at 450 degrees for 12 to 15 minutes.

    These are delicious with Herbed Tomato Soup and many other dishes as well. These biscuits can be given in a gift basket as a mix. To make the mix, simply leave out the milk. Mix everything else together and put it in a zip lock bag along with the recipe and instructions for using the mix.

HIGH COUNTRY HERBS

Lemon Poppy Seed Bread
Makes 1 Loaf

2 1/2 cups flour

1 Tbs. baking powder

3/4 tsp. salt

3/4 cup sugar

1 Tbs. poppy seeds

2 tsp. grated lemon rind

4 Tbs. butter

1 cup milk

1/2 cup vegetable oil

1 egg

1/4 cup lemon juice

Mix sugar, butter, egg and oil until creamed. Add lemon juice, milk, lemon rind, and poppy seed. Add salt, flour and baking powder. Mix well. Grease pans. Pour into 4 small bread pans, 1 large bread pan, or a 12 muffin pan. Bake at 350 degrees for 45 to 55 minutes. This bread is a great at breakfast, or as a treat to share with friends at work.

HIGH COUNTRY HERBS

Orange Bread
Makes 1 Loaf
This bread is a lot of work, but it is well worth the trouble.
It is a great addition to an English Tea basket.

Rind of 4 oranges, finely chopped

4 cups of sugar

1/4 cup butter

2 large eggs

2 cups milk

6 cups flour

4 tsp. baking powder

2 tsp. salt

Place chopped orange rind and 2 cups water in a small saucepan, bring to boil, simmer for 15 minutes. Add sugar and simmer 30 more minutes. Add butter. Remove from heat and let cool completely.

In a large bowl combine eggs and milk, add cooled orange mixture. Add flour, salt and baking powder. Stir until smooth. Pour into small greased baking pans or muffin tins. Bake at 350 degrees for 45 to 60 minutes, until toothpick inserted in center comes out clean. Cool in pans for 10 minutes. Remove from pans and let cool completely on a rack.

HIGH COUNTRY HERBS

Scone Mix
Makes about Two Dozen
I try to keep this mix in my refrigerator at all times.

4 cups flour

4 Tbs. sugar

4 tsp. baking powder

1 tsp. baking soda

1 tsp. salt

12 Tbs. cold butter

4 Tbs. powdered buttermilk

1 cup currants or hazelnuts or dried cranberries
or
whatever desired dried fruit or nuts, or for
a sweeter treat, try chocolate chips!

To make scones, mix 1 1/4 cups mix, 1 large egg, and 1/4 cup water. Combine and mix as little as possible to blend. Dump out on floured surface, knead gently and form into a round about 1/2 inch thick. Place on ungreased baking sheet. Score into wedges, but don't cut all the way through. Bake at 425 degrees for about 12 minutes.

Or you can just drop the dough onto a cookie sheet,

slightly flatten them and bake as directed above.

This makes a great gift with a jar of homemade jelly. Put enough to make one batch of scones into a zip lock bag. Copy the recipe onto a recipe card to include in the basket. Buy a jar of lemon curd or orange marmalade if you don't make jelly. If you want more in the basket, add some tea, a nice mug and maybe a pretty cloth napkin.

HIGH COUNTRY HERBS

The Spreads

HIGH COUNTRY HERBS

The Spreads

Okay, you planted all those little packages of seeds you bought last spring and of course, they grew into a lush, wonderful garden of herbs. You picked, washed, dried, diced, chopped, puréed, and mixed your little heart out and now you have a cupboard and freezer full of deliciousness just waiting to be combined with your culinary talents.

The hard frost hit last week and you have the garden cleaned off and put to bed for the winter. You finally pulled out the bread machine you got for Mother's Day, that you haven't had time to try what with all the growing and gardening and making of seasonings that you have been doing. So today you baked a loaf of Roasted Red Pepper Bread and you have a kettle of homemade soup simmering on the stove. (We don't know what kind of soup yet because we haven't gotten to that chapter.) Your family is already looking healthier just from all the wonderful aromas floating through the house.

The bread is sitting on a wire rack cooling and you get out the bowls to dish up the soup. Now are you really going to grab that tub of soft margarine from the refrigerator to spread on this wonder you've created? Or do you want something that will be equal to the bread? If you do, here are some suggestions:

HIGH COUNTRY HERBS

Quick Herb Dip
If you don't have much time try this:

Pour a little olive oil (a good grade of olive oil is lightly green in color) into a shallow dish, stir in about a teaspoon of crushed garlic (remember, you have that ready in a jar in the refrigerator right beside the grated ginger), add a sprinkle of Italian Seasoning and a tablespoon or two of grated Parmesan, Asiago, or Romano cheese. Slice off pieces of bread and dip the chunks into this nectar of the Gods.

Or stir a couple of tablespoons of your chopped frozen Chives into some butter. (Remember, fat is fat and it is better to have natural butter than the hydrogenated oils found in margarine.) If you want something a little fancier, add a teaspoon of crushed garlic or Horseradish, 1/4 cup of cheese, and a dash of hot pepper sauce. Now you really have a flavor that will match your bread.

HIGH COUNTRY HERBS

Tapenade
Makes about 1 Cup

This black olive paste is a staple in Provençe in the winter. You can spread it on crackers, use it as a vegetable dip, stuff eggs with it, or serve it over pasta. You can also spread it on your homemade bread.

1 cup pitted black olives
> (some should be Greek olives if you can find them.)

3 or 4 cloves of garlic, crushed

1 can of anchovies, rinsed and drained
or
a small can of albacore tuna, drained well.

1/4 cup chopped fresh or frozen basil (or a couple of cubes of your basil pesto)

1/4 to 1/2 cup of olive oil

Place all the ingredients, except the olive oil, into a food processor. Process until smooth, then slowly add the olive oil until it is the right consistency and taste for your palette. You can store it in a jar in the refrigerator for up to a month, if it lasts that long. (But it won't!)

HIGH COUNTRY HERBS

Pestos for Dips & Spreads

As I already told you, (see page 35) you can mix your pestos with cottage cheese, cream cheese, mayonnaise, plain yogurt or sour cream, or a combination of any two of them. You can add diced tomatoes, diced green chilies, chopped scallions, sunflower seeds, chopped pine nuts or pecans, chopped olives, diced avocado and/or shredded cheese to any of these to make a delicious spread for bread. Remember we are going for healthy food as well as food with great flavor.

HIGH COUNTRY HERBS

Red Bell Pepper Purée
Makes about 1 Cup

You can also make a red bell pepper purée that you can freeze and use for dips, spreads, pizza sauce, salad dressing or pasta sauce. Here is how you do it. This, too, is a staple in my kitchen.

Start with 6 big red bell peppers, wash them well and dry them.

Lay them on a grill or under a broiler until the skins are blistered and blackened. Place the charred peppers in a bowl you can cover with a plate or in a paper bag and let them cool. When they are cool, they will peel easily. After they are peeled, cut the peppers in half, remove the seeds and cut them into strips. You can stop right here and put them in bags and freeze them. Or you can peel a medium sized onion, slice it and cook it in a little olive oil until it is limp and clear. Let it cool a bit, then put the onion in the food processor or blender with the red pepper strips and four cloves of garlic, a dash of balsamic vinegar, and a tablespoon of dried Parsley. (Or two tablespoons of fresh Parsley) and process or blend until smooth.

Pour into ice cube trays and freeze. When the purée is frozen, put the cubes into a plastic bag and store in the freezer until needed. You can use it to make spreads in exactly the same way you use the pesto. Use your imagination and you will come up with something delicious.

HIGH COUNTRY HERBS

Baba Ghanoush
Makes about 2 Cups

No party can be complete without a savory dish of this wonderful spread. It is easy to make, very low fat, low calorie, and versatile. What more can you ask of a spread?

1 pound eggplants, any variety.

Poke the eggplants in several places with a fork. Line a baking sheet with foil and spray with olive oil. Lay the egplants on the foil and bake at 400 degrees for 30 to 50 minutes or until they are uniformly soft. Remove from the oven and allow to cool. (You may also grill them on a gas grill on high, which takes about 15 to 25 minutes.)

While the eggplants are cooking, sauté 1 finely chopped small onion in a tablespoon of olive oil until lightly browned. Let cool.

When the eggplants are cool, cut them in half and using a spoon, scoop out the insides and place in a colander to drain. Let the pulp drain about 5 to 10 minutes. Then put the pulp in a food processor.

Add:

1 1/2 tsp. lemon juice

1 clove of garlic

1 Tbs. of tahini paste (this is sesame paste, which you can get at a health food store)

or

1 Tbs. mayonnaise or 1 Tbs. peanut butter

1 1/2 tsp. olive oil

1 tsp. fresh parsley **or** 1/2 tsp. dried parsley

Process everything lightly, until the mixture has a coarse, roughly chopped texture.

Pour into a bowl and stir in the onion. Add freshly ground pepper to taste. Chill for at least 60 minutes before serving.

Use Baba Ghanoush as a spread for bread or crackers, or a dip for pita chips. Use two or three tablespoons as a topping for salad. If you have never eaten eggplant, try it this way. I am sure you will like it. This is always a big hit at parties in my home.

White Bean Herb Spread
Makes about 2 Cups
You may use this as a dip or spread, or use it to stuff eggs.

2 cups cooked white beans
or
1 - 15 ounce can rinsed and drained

2 Tbs. olive oil

1 Tbs. balsamic vinegar

2 cloves garlic, minced (or more, to taste)

1/4 cup chopped fresh parsley **or** 2 Tbs. dried

1 Tbs. minced fresh rosemary **or** 1 tsp. dried, crumbled

1/3 cup finely diced celery

dash of hot pepper sauce

freshly ground pepper

Mash the beans and stir in the rest of the ingredients. Cool for at least 30 minutes, then taste and adjust the seasoning if need be. Keep refrigerated. Allow to come to room temperature before serving.

HIGH COUNTRY HERBS

Salsa
Makes about 3 1/2 Cups

You can quickly peel tomatoes by dipping them into boiling water for a few minutes, or if you are using firm garden tomatoes, rub the blade of your knife over the outside of the tomato. This will loosen the skin and you can peel it easily. You can also freeze whole tomatoes and run them under hot water. The skins will come right off. Then dice the tomato and use it in this dish or in cooked dishes. Use whatever hot peppers you like in the recipe. If you add the seeds of the peppers, the salsa will be hotter.

1 -15 oz can diced tomatoes
or
3 fresh tomatoes peeled and diced

1 small onion diced
or
2 Tbs. dried minced onion
or
6 green onions diced

1 can diced green chilies
or
2 jalapeños
or
Anaheim peppers, seeded and diced

1 red or green bell pepper, seeded and diced (optional)

1 avocado, peeled and diced (optional)

1 cucumber, peeled, seeded and diced (optional)

1 Tbs. chopped parsley or cilantro

1 clove garlic, minced

1/4 tsp. cumin

1 Tbs. lime juice

1/2 tsp. oregano (optional)

Mix all together and serve with any Mexican food, as a dip for chips. It also makes a great topping with cheese on a baked potato.

Salsa Verde
Makes about 1 Cup

3 cloves garlic minced

1 large onion diced

1 Tbs. lime juice

12 fresh tomatillos, husked and finely chopped

1 can diced green chilies
or
2 jalapeños
or
Anaheim peppers, seeded and diced

1 Tbs. chopped parsley or coriander

hot sauce to taste

Mix all the ingredients together. Allow the flavors to blend. You may also add avocado to this salsa or red bell peppers diced add a nice color. This dip may be made ahead and frozen.

Tomatillo grows very well here. They have a culture similar to tomatoes being considered a husk tomato because the fruit is contained in a husk. When the husk dries, the fruit is ready to be picked. These are also readily available at most groceries, at least in our area, and in farmers' markets.

HIGH COUNTRY HERBS

The Soups

HIGH COUNTRY HERBS

Soups

Nothing is any easier to make than homemade soup. You can use canned or frozen foods to make an especially quick soup if you don't have time to peel, slice and dice your own vegetables. Canned broths may be used, but you will need to watch the salt content and the preservatives. Most canned chicken products as well as most bouillon cubes contain MSG and other undesirable preservatives.

Making your own stock is easy, but time consuming. You can make beef, chicken or vegetable stock very easily and freeze it in containers for later use. If you want to use canned stock or broth, find the healthiest alternative you can.

Soup is filling and warming on a cold winter day. Soup is generally low fat and low in calories, especially vegetable soups. Creamed soups made at home can be low fat when made with my delicious recipes. Soup is medicinal! Even the aroma of a kettle of soup cooking makes me feel well, loved, warm and happy.

In the summer when it is too hot to eat, try a cold soup. If you have never eaten cold soup, you are in for a real taste treat. A bowl of Gazpacho, a slice of garlic cheese bread spread with

Baba Ghanoush or tapenade makes a simple gourmet meal on a hot summer evening.

Some of these soups are old standbys and some may be new to you. Life is an adventure! Try teh new ones!

So let's begin making our soup. Since the base of many of our soups will be chicken or beef stock, we'll begin with how to make a great stock.

Beef or Chicken Broth (Stock)
Makes about 8 Cups

3-4 lb. of beef bones or chicken wings, necks, or backs. Spray a Dutch oven or a heavy pan with Pam or any spray of your choice. Set the oven temperature at 400 degrees. Place the bones or chicken parts in the Dutch Oven and cook for 1 to 1 1/2 hours, until they are well browned, but not burned. Remove from oven and cover with water. Add an onion cut into chunks, a carrot, a stalk of celery, and 2 cloves of garlic, crushed.

Cover and simmer 2-3 hours or until meat is very tender. Strain broth and refrigerate. The fat will congeal on the top of the broth. Remove the fat and discard. Freeze the broth in pints or quarts until ready to use. Pick meat from bones, discarding fat and skin. Add it to the broth or save it for another use.

HIGH COUNTRY HERBS

Herbed Fresh Tomato Soup
This serves 4 people generously

1/2 cup onion, diced

1/4 cup celery, diced

1/4 cup carrots, diced

2 cloves garlic, minced

2 Tbs. olive

1 bay leaf

1/4 cup minced fresh parsley **or** 2 Tbs. dried

1/2 tsp. dried thyme

1/2 tsp. dried marjoram

2 tsp. dried basil

4 cups chicken stock

8 to 10 large tomatoes, peeled and diced,
or
2 pints canned tomatoes, preferably home canned
or

the equivalent of frozen tomatoes

Sauté onion, carrots, celery, and garlic in olive oil until soft and lightly browned. Add herbs and tomatoes. Cook about 10 minutes. Stir in stock and simmer for 15 to 20 minutes. The recipe can be easily halved for two people.

Bean Chowder
Serves 4

I made this recipe when I was tired of chili and tired of bean soup
and just plain wanted something different!

1 cup dried beans, soaked overnight and cooked
      until soft

or

two 15 ounce cans of Great Northern beans, rinsed
      and drained

1 medium onion chopped

2 jalapeños seeded and diced

or

1 can of diced green chilies

1 green pepper seeded and diced (optional)

1 stalk celery, diced

1 lb. bulk sausage or hamburger, browned

2 cloves garlic, crushed

1/2 tsp. thyme

1 tsp. savory

1/2 tsp. dry mustard

1/2 tsp. ground allspice

2 - 14 1/2 oz. cans tomato sauce

2 cups beef or chicken broth

salt and lemon pepper to taste

Brown meat and garlic in a heavy skillet or Dutch oven. Add vegetables and cook until lightly browned and limp. Stir in herbs, tomato sauce, broth and beans. Simmer until heated through. Adjust seasonings as needed. You can also add 1 cup diced potato, if desired. Serve with cornbread or a hearty whole wheat bread for a full meal.

Wild Rice Soup
Serves 4

This is a decicious soup for a cold winter day. If you can't find wild rice use brown but not white. Remember that most white foods have all of the nutrients processed out of them.

4 cups beef broth

1/4 cup wild rice

1 clove garlic, minced

1/4 cup carrot, diced

1/4 cup celery, diced

1/4 cup onion, diced

1 to 2 cups mushrooms, diced

1 Tbs. parsley

1/2 tsp. seasoning salt

1/4 tsp. thyme

1/4 tsp. poultry seasoning

lemon pepper

1 bay leaf

1 Tbs. olive oil

Bring 2 cups of broth to a boil and stir in wild rice. Cover, lower heat to simmer and cook for 50 minutes or until rice is done. Meantime, lightly brown vegetables in a heavy skillet in olive oil. Stir vegetables into rice. Add the other two cups of broth. Add seasonings and let simmer until flavors blend. Adjust seasonings as necessary. Serve hot with bread.

Basic Cream Soup
Serves 4
This is a very versitile recipe and a baase for a number
of cream soups and chowders.

4 slices of bacon, fried and crumbled
or
1 Tbs. olive oil

1/4 onion,diced
or
1 Tbs. onion flakes

1/2 stalk celery, diced

1/4 cup carrot, peeled and diced

1 clove garlic

1 Tbs. chopped parsley

2 cups of any vegetables you choose
(cabbage, cauliflower, broccoli, corn, potatoes,
mushrooms, in any combination depending on
the type of soup you're making)

2 cups broth, chicken, vegetable or beef

1 Tbs. flour

1 can evaporated skim or fat-free milk

or
2 cups whole milk
or
2 cups of half and half

Salt and pepper to taste

Cook bacon in a heavy skillet or pan until well browned. Remove bacon to paper towel to cool. Reserve 1 Tbs. of bacon grease, discarding the rest.

Use reserved bacon grease or olive oil in a heavy pan or skillet. Stir in onions, garlic, carrot, and celery into the hot oil or bacon grease and cook until lightly browned and limp. Stir the 2 cups vegetables into the same pan. Stir and cook until well blended. Add the broth and simmer until vegetables are done. Mix flour with a little of the milk, stirring until smooth. Stir this into the soup, add rest of milk, and simmer until slightly thickened. Mix in crumbled bacon if you are using bacon.

For cabbage, cauliflower, potato, or broccoli soup you can add 2 to 4 slices of cheese if you wish. Or add a little diced red pepper to the corn for corn chowder. Or add a can of minced clams to the potato soup for clam chowder. For mushroom soup I like to use 2 or 3 different kinds of mushrooms.

You can also add 1 cup of diced turkey, chicken, ham, salmon or any other meat you think might taste good.

Mulligatawny Soup
Serves 6

1 1/4 lb. chicken thighs or legs (about 8)

8 cups water

1 Tbs. olive oil

2 cloves garlic, minced

1 medium yellow onion, peeled and chopped

2 stalks celery, chopped

1 1/2 cups chopped carrots

2 1/2 tsp. curry powder or to taste

2 tsp. salt

Brown chicken thighs in 350 degree oven for 1 hour. Remove and add water. Cover and simmer until chicken is tender. Remove the chicken from the stock, cool, debone and chop the meat. Put chopped meat back in stock. In a large skillet, heat olive oil and sauté garlic, onion, celery, and carrots until lightly browned and tender. Stir the vegetables into the stock and meat. Add remaining ingredients and cook about 30 minutes, covered, until flavors are blended. Serve hot, either as a main dish with a good bread, or as a soup to begin the meal.

HIGH COUNTRY HERBS

Pasta Fagiole
Serves 4

1/2 cup carrots, diced

1/4 cup celery, diced

1/2 cup onion, diced

1 clove garlic, minced

1 Tbs. olive oil

1 can white beans

1 can
or
2 cups of any kind of broth

1/2 cup dry shell macaroni

1 Tbs. dried parsley

Heat olive oil in a heavy skillet or pan. Add carrots, celery, onion and garlic. Cook until lightly browned. Add broth. Cover and cook until vegetables are tender. Add beans, pasta and parsley. Cook uncovered 12 to 15 minutes until pasta is done. Serve hot with foccacia for a good Italian meal. Add some slices of cheese and salami for a complete meal.

HIGH COUNTRY HERBS

Gazpacho
Serves 2 Generously, 4 as an Appetizer
This is so good on a hot summer evening or for lunch after
spending the morning in the garden.

3 large tomatoes, peeled, cored and diced
or
4 cups of canned or frozen tomatoes

1 red or green bell pepper, seeded and diced (optional)

1/2 a small sweet onion, such as Vidalia
or
2 to 4 shallots or scallions, peeled and diced

2 cloves garlic, minced

Salt and pepper to taste

2 to 3 cups of broth
or
tomato juice
or
a combination of the two

Dash of hot pepper sauce (optional)

Diced avocado for garnish (optional)

2 tsp. lime or lemon juice or salt

1/3 cup sherry (optional)

You may also add 1 stalk of diced celery or a small diced cucumber if desired. Chill the soup thoroughly and serve cold with a dollop of sour cream or guacamole.

Cold Shrimp & Avocado Soup
Serves 4
This is so good you wouldn't believe me,
even if I tried to tell you!

1 pound small shrimp

1 Tbs. olive oil

2 cloves minced garlic

2 to 4 shallots
or
1/2 medium red onion
or
4 to 6 scallions, peeled and diced

1 Tbs. fresh parsley or chives, chopped

Heat the oil in a skillet, add the garlic, and onion, shallots or scallions, and cook until lightly browned. Stir in shrimp and cook until shrimp are pink.

Remove from heat and stir in 3 to 4 cups of broth and chives or parsley. Chicken or vegetable is best. Chill the soup.

Put one serving of soup into a bowl. Add 1/4 of an avocado, peeled and diced. You may also add a tablespoon of diced tomato for garnish if desired. Serve this with a French type baguette, with a red pepper spread made with red pepper pesto and creamed cheese, with a little chopped chives stirred in.

HIGH COUNTRY HERBS

Avegolomano
(Icy Lemon Soup)
Serves 6
This Greek soup is delicious and refreshing in hot weather

6 cups chicken broth

3 eggs

1/4 cup long grain rice

1 tsp. salt

1/2 cup fresh lemon juice

1 lemon, thinly sliced

Combine broth, rice and salt in a large sauce pan. Cover and bring to a boil and simmer until rice is tender (about 15 minutes). Remove from heat.

In a bowl beat the eggs until fluffy and pale yellow. Beat in lemon juice. Slowly stir about 2 cups of the hot broth into the egg mixture and wisk vigorously. Pour all back into the soup and wisk until slightly thickened. Cool to room temperature then chill. The soup will thicken as it chills. Garnish with lemon slices and serve.

HIGH COUNTRY HERBS

The Seasonings

HIGH COUNTRY HERBS

The Seasonings

Your garden is growing well, with big healthy plants ready to harvest and you want to begin cooking with them so let's start with some recipes for seasoning mixes. I should tell you at the beginning that these seasonings should come with the warning label, "Can be Addictive." Once you start using these in your cooking, you may not be able to go back to the bland seasonings you can buy commercially.

Seasoning Salt Mix
Makes about 1 Cup

3/4 cup sea salt

1 Tbs. garlic powder

1 tsp. ground black pepper

1/2 tsp. dried oregano

1/8 tsp. turmeric

1 Tbs. onion powder

1/4 tsp. dry mustard

1/4 tsp. white pepper

1/8 tsp. celery seed

1 tsp. paprika

1 Tbs. dried parsley

Mix all ingredients together making sure the leaves are crushed and well distributed and store in a jar.

A nice shaker filled with this salt along with another shaker of lemon pepper in a small basket makes a gift that anyone will enjoy.

The first time I made this seasoning, I thought it tasted a lot like most of the commercial seasoning salts that you can buy. Then we went camping and my husband and friends caught some fish. We decided to cook them on the grill. When I went to get my seasoning salt, I found I had forgotten it at home. So I ran into town and bought the commercial stuff, figuring it would be just as good. Wrong. This was the first time it was really brought home to me that freshly made seasonings do taste better.

Lemon Pepper Seasoning Mix
Makes about 2 Cups
This is much more flavorful than anything
you can buy commercially.

1 cup ground black pepper

1/4 cup dried minced onion

1/3 cup dried lemon peel

1/4 cup dried thyme leaves

1 tsp. oregano

2 tsp. cumin

2 tsp. garlic powder

2 tsp. paprika

1/4 tsp. cayenne

2 tsp. citric acid (optional)

2 tsp. onion powder

Mix all the ingredients together. I like to put the onion through my coffee grinder. I usually add the thyme, oregano and lemon peel and grind it to a fine powder.   Use it anywhere you would normally use pepper.   If you only try two of these seasonings, I would be sure to make this and the seasoning salt.

I think you will be pleasantly surprised at the taste even if all you use it on is a hamburger.   You will find that lemon pepper and seasoning salt are used throughout the book in all kinds of recipes.

Poultry Seasoning Mix
Makes about 1/2 Cup
This is excellent on all birds. Try it with a little white wine
and lemon juice on pheasant!

4 tsp. dried marjoram

4 tsp. onion powder

2 tsp. dried thyme

2 tsp. dried sage

2 tsp. dried savory

1 tsp. celery seed

1 tsp. white pepper

4 tsp. parsley

Mix all together and either grind with a mortar and pestle or put everything in your coffee grinder and mix it well. This seasoning is good in stuffing, on fried chicken, and in chicken soup.

HIGH COUNTRY HERBS

Italian Seasoning
Makes about 1 Cup
This is good on so many things. Try it on a little garlic bread
before toasting under the broiler. Also great on tomato salad!

4 Tbs. dried oregano

4 Tbs. dried basil

2 tsp. dried rosemary

1 tsp. garlic powder

1 tsp. onion powder

1/2 tsp. lemon pepper

4 tsp. dried thyme

4 tsp. fennel seed

4 Tbs. dried parsley

1/4 tsp. dried cloves

1/2 tsp. celery seed

1/4 tsp. dried lovage (optional)

4 whole bay leaves crushed

Place all ingredients in a small food processor and process lightly until well mixed. This seasoning is good with all Italian dishes and anything with tomatoes, such as Herbed Tomato Soup (in the Soup section of the book.)

Chili Powder
Makes about 1/4 Cup
This is essential for making Barbeque Rub.

4 dried hot chili peppers (seeds removed if desired)
or
2 tsp. crushed red pepper

2 Tbs. ground cumin

2 tsp. dried oregano

2 tsp. garlic powder

2 tsp. onion powder

1 tsp. ground allspice

1/8 tsp. cloves

You may want to grow and dry your own chilies for this mix. If you do, I recommend Serrano, Anaheim, or whatever hot pepper plant you can find at your local greenhouse. I would stay away from Habenero, unless you really like it hot. Jalapeños are good chilies to grow for salsas and cooking, but they don't dry particularly well.

If you prefer not to grow your own peppers, most groceries carry at least crushed red pepper, if not dried peppers in several varieties. I like to use several different kinds of peppers, as I think a variety gives the best flavor. This Chili Powder is essential to making the babecue seasoning that follows. And, of course, it is used to flavor Chili Con Carne and Green Chili as well as being used in the Black and Red Chili Mix.

Put all the ingredients in the coffee grinder and grind it to a powder. Use sparingly until you determine the heat of your product, as heat varies from chili pepper to chili pepper and even from season to season. Remember, you can always add more, but once it's in you can't take it out.

Barbeque Rub
Makes about 1/2 Cup

2 Tbs. chili powder

2 Tbs. dry mustard

1 Tbs. paprika

1 Tbs. garlic powder

1 Tbs. ground cumin

1/2 tsp. cayenne pepper

1/2 tsp. ground cloves

Place all ingredients in an herb grinder or a mini processor and process until well mixed. This seasoning is great on steaks, hamburgers, chicken or pork chops. Rub it into the meat and grill it, bake it or flour and fry it, if that is your choice.

HIGH COUNTRY HERBS

Meat Rub
Makes about 3/4 Cup
This is excellent seasoning for game meat but also
works well on beef and pork.

2 Tbs. ground cumin

2 Tbs. garlic powder

2 Tbs. dried onion

2 Tbs. brown sugar

2 Tbs. paprika

1 Tbs. ground coriander

2 tsp salt

1 tsp pepper

1 tsp oregano

1 tsp thyme

1 tsp crushed red pepper flakes

1 tsp mustard powder

1 tsp fennel seed

1 tsp dried basil

Grind seeds and dried onion in your grinder. Mix together with the other ingredients. Rub on meat, then grill, roast, sauté or broil. This Meat Rub is very different than the Barbeque Rub and you might find it more to your liking if you don't like things quite so spicy.

No Salt Seasoning Mix
Makes about 1/4 Cup
Perfect if you are trying to cut down on your salt intake.
You won't believe the flavor!

1/2 tsp. garlic powder

1/4 tsp. dry mustard

1/4 tsp. thyme leaves

1/4 tsp. dried lemon peel

1/4 tsp. onion powder

1/4 tsp. ground black pepper

1/4 tsp. paprika

1/8 tsp. celery seed

1/4 tsp. white pepper

1 Tbs. citric acid

1 Tbs. dried cilantro **or** parsley

Blend all together in mini food processor until well powdered. You may not be on a low salt diet, but you might have a friend or relative who is. This is a delicious salt substitute without any preservatives or MSG. I would recommend this for anyone who wants or needs to cut down on salt consumption.

Curry Powder
Makes about 1/4 Cup
This is a mild curry rather than a spicy one.
It makes a nice addition to rice dishes.

2 tsp. cinnamon

1/2 tsp. ground cardamom

1/2 tsp. ground cloves

3 tsp. ground cumin

1 tsp. pepper

1/2 tsp. ground coriander

1 tsp. turmeric

2 tsp. ground fenugreek
> (this is very hard to find unless you grow it yourself, so you
> can substitute fennel or anise seed))

1 tsp. cayenne or to taste

Feel free to grind your own spices for this. Use your grinder and grind whole cinnamon, cloves, cumin seeds, pepper corns, coriander and fenugreek, fennel or anise seeds. You will be surprised at what a difference fresh ground spices will make in flavor. Curry Powder is used to season meat dishes. Curry comes in many varieties, some are very spicy and some are mild. This particular version is quite mild. You may also use Curry as a rub on meat before baking or grilling it.

Indian Masala
Makes about 1/3 Cup

There are probably as many variations of curry powder
as there are cooks. This is a spicier version
than the last but still relatively mild.

2 1/2 Tbs. paprika

1 Tbs. ground coriander

1 Tbs. ground cumin

3/4 tsp. pepper

1/2 tsp. ground cinnamon

1/2 tsp. ground ginger

1/2 tsp. ground turmeric

1/4 tsp. cayenne pepper

Mix together. Use as a rub for poultry, vegetables, pork
or beef, then roast or grill. Masala is one of the many varieties of
Curry Powder. You might also want to use this seasoning in the
Mulligatawny Soup. (recipe found in the soup chapter)

HIGH COUNTRY HERBS

Turkey Baste
Makes about 3/4 Cup
If you don't try anything else in this book, try this.
I never cook any poultry without it.

1/4 tsp. dry mustard

1 tsp. fennel seed

1/4 tsp. nutmeg

1 tsp. pepper

1/4 tsp. allspice

2 tsp. dried parsley

1 tsp. sage

2 Tbs. lemon juice

1/2 cup white wine such as Chablis
> (Use a good wine that you would enjoy drinking. Do not use cooking wine. Cooking wine is loaded with salt and it is usually a poor quality wine in the first place.)

Grind herbs together with a mortar, then mix with wine and lemon juice. Generously brush inside of turkey and stuff as usual. Brush outside with remainder of baste at beginning and several times during baking.

HIGH COUNTRY HERBS

Although this is called Turkey Baste it can be used to baste and flavor any poultry. It makes a very good, flavorful, moist meat, whatever it is used on. I have used it for wild turkey, pheasant, chicken, Cornish game hen, as well as turkey.

This is a great gift for a meat seasoning basket when paired with the Barbeque Rub, Poultry Seasoning and Fish Seasoning.

Fish Seasoning
Makes about 1/2 Cup
This is similar to Old Bay Seasoning but better.
Tiy can use it for boiling lobster or steaming clams
as well as cooking fish.

1 1/2 Tbs. celery seed

1/2 tsp. ground ginger

1 1/2 Tbs. salt

1 Tbs. paprika

1 Tbs. black pepper

1 to 2 tsp. cayenne

1/2 Tbs. dry mustard

1/2 Tbs. thyme

2 whole bay leaves, crushed

Use the grinder to grind the celery seed, thyme, and bay leaves to a powder. Mix well with the other ingredients. You can mix a tablespoon of this with 1/2 cup corn meal (or corn flour, if you can find it) and 1/2 cup flour for a delicious fish coating for fried fish. It is very good in shrimp scampi or when used to season bay scallops.

HIGH COUNTRY HERBS

Preserved Ginger
Makes about 1 Cup

Peel and thinly slice or grate 2 large fresh ginger roots. (I do mine in the food processor.) Put in a jar and cover with rice wine, *sake*, or dry sherry. Keep in refrigerator. This is really handy to have on hand for Chinese cooking and it will keep for a very long time. You will find it included in many of these recipes.

HIGH COUNTRY HERBS

Chinese Five Spice Powder
Makes about 1/4 Cup
This mix gives a very authentic flavor to Chinese recipes.

2 tsp. anise seed **or** star anise

2 tsp. fennel seed

2 tsp. peppercorns

2 tsp. whole cloves

1 stick cinnamon about 2 inches long

Put all ingredients in a spice grinder or coffee grinder and grind until fine. Use to season meat for stir frying. This is so much better than what you can buy, it is well worth the effort. And you might want to make a Chinese gift basket with this, plus Plum Sauce, grated Ginger, Stir Fry Sauce and a jar of rice. Include some chopsticks and Oolong tea.

HIGH COUNTRY HERBS

Plum Sauce
Makes about 3 Cups
This is a great dipping sauce if you don't care for hot mustard.

1 lb. red or purple plums quartered, pitted, and chopped.

1/2 cup firmly packed brown sugar

1/3 cup water

1 Tbs. soy sauce

1 tsp. freshly grated ginger root

1 tsp. salt

1/3 cup catsup

1 tsp. lemon juice

Mix all together and bring to boil in heavy saucepan. Reduce heat and cook 10 to 15 minutes. Pour into a food processor and process until smooth. Serve with Chinese food such as eggrolls.

HIGH COUNTRY HERBS

Stir Fry Sauce
Makes about 1 Quart
This can be used as a marinade for any
kind of meat prior to grilling.

1 cup honey

1 cup soy sauce

1 cup *sake* **or** dry sherry

1/4 cup ginger
> (use some from the jar of grated ginger you now have in
> your refrigerator)

Mix all together and use 1/4 cup to marinate meats for stir frying. Marinate for at least 1/2 hour. Then fry the meat, throw in some vegetables and cook until tender/crisp, about 5 minutes. Mix 1 cup of chicken broth and 2 Tbs. of cornstarch, pour over meat and vegetables and cook until clear and thickened. Serve over rice or Chinese noodles.

HIGH COUNTRY HERBS

Pumpkin Pie Spice
Makes about 2 Tbs.
When I tell people I use the recipe off the pumpkin filling can
they never believe me. That's how much difference
fresh ground seasonings can make!

2 tsp. ground nutmeg

2 tsp. ground cinnamon

1 tsp. ground ginger

1/2 tsp. ground mace

1/2 tsp. ground cloves

1/2 tsp. ground allspice

Fresh whole spices ground make the best seasoning. Even
spices that are already ground will make a better seasoning than
any pumpkin pie spice you can buy.

HIGH COUNTRY HERBS

Mediterranean Herb Salad Mix
Makes about 1/4 Cup
This is a great addition sprinkled on a salad
or a good basis for a vinegrette.

1 Tbs. dried parsley

1 Tbs. dried onion

2 Tbs. dried basil

1 1/2 tsp. garlic powder

1 1/2 tsp. lemon pepper

Sprinkle over green salads as you mix, or to make an herb dressing, combine 2 Tbs. of herb mix, 1 Tbs. sugar or honey (optional), 1/4 cup wine vinegar and 1/2 cup olive oil.

HIGH COUNTRY HERBS

The Salads
&
Salad Dressings

HIGH COUNTRY HERBS

The Salads & Salad Dressings

As long as you are raising herbs, why not tuck in a row or two of salad greens? A row of New Zealand Spinach perhaps, beside a row of Mesclun, which is lettuces mixed with other greens, would be good for your first garden. Add a tomato plant or two. Something like an Early Girl or a Patio tomato have short seasons so you will probably get ripe tomatoes, even in our climate.

Shallots are planted from bulbs and need to be put in either in the fall or as early in the spring as the ground can be worked, around the middle of March in most years.

Onions for scallions may be planted quite early, usually by mid-April to the first part of May. Be sure to use your soil thermometer to check soil temperatures before planting. If the ground is not warm enough, the seed or bulbs will not sprout and may rot.

You might want to try some fingerling carrots, a broccoli plant or two, a bush cucumber, and a couple of bell pepper plants. This should make a nice salad garden along with your herbs.

Of course you can buy these things from the market or the farmers' market if you don't want to grow them yourself.

When you have nice fresh vegetables from your garden,

why not make a fresh salad dressing for it, rather than a bottled one full of all those things you can't pronounce and don't even know why they are in the dressing? And there is the question I always ask myself: if I don't know what it is or what it does, do I really want to put it in my body?

A Simple Salad
Serves 6

Traditional salad dressings have 3 parts oil to 1 part vinegar. Dressings made with pestos generally use a little more vinegar than oil, because the pesto is already made with oil. You can make a simple, yet delicious salad with alternating slices of red onion, tomatoes, and mozzarella cheese topped with a basil pesto vinaigrette.

Slice 3 - 4 tomatoes, peel and slice the onion, and slice the cheese. Lay them in alternating layers around a plate.

Now mix 3 Tbs. wine vinegar, 1 Tbs. pesto with 6 Tbs. of good olive oil. Add salt and freshly ground pepper to taste. Tuck a few whole basil leaves around the plate. Give the vinaigrette a final stir and drizzle it over the platter. Add some chopped chives, parsley and/or chervil for garnish.

HIGH COUNTRY HERBS

Lemon or Lime Vinaigrette
Makes 1 Cup

2 Tbs. wine vinegar
or
1 Tbs. wine vinegar and 1 Tbs. of lemon **or** lime juice

1 Tbs. lemon or lime zest

6 Tbs. extra-virgin olive oil

3 Tbs. chopped parsley, chervil, basil, or chives, **or** a
combination. (Cilantro is especially good with lime)

1/2 tsp. Dijon mustard

1 tsp. honey

1 Tbs. pickled nasturtium seeds **or** capers (optional)

Salt and freshly ground pepper to taste

Mix together with a whisk. Whisk once again before
drizzling over salad.

HIGH COUNTRY HERBS

Garlic Vinaigrette
Makes 1 Cup

3 to 4 cloves of garlic, minced

3/4 cup olive oil

1/4 cup wine vinegar or herbed vinegar
(part lemon juice is nice or part balsamic vinegar)

1 tsp. sugar

Salt and freshly ground pepper to taste

Minced herbs to taste
Chives, parsley, chervil, rosemary or basil would all go well
in this vinaigrette.

Put everything in a jar with a tight fitting lid, and shake well. You can store this in the refrigerator for about a week. Use it for salad dressing or brush it on chicken that you are grilling or use it as a marinade for other meat.

HIGH COUNTRY HERBS

Spinach Salad
Serves 4

1 lb. fresh spinach, stems removed, washed and drained

1 Tbs. fresh chives, chopped

1 large red onion, diced

1/2 lb. bacon, chopped, browned, and drained, reserving 1 Tbs. drippings

1/3 cup rice wine vinegar

2 Tbs. honey

1/3 cup apple juice

2 Tbs. Dijon mustard

1/2 cup pine nuts toasted

1/2 cup corn, either canned **or** fresh that has been cooked and cut from the cob

Fry bacon and onion until bacon is crisp and onion is limp. Drain, reserving 1 Tbs. drippings in a pan with bacon and onions. Remove the bacon and stir the vinegar, honey, apple juice, and Dijon into the pan. Simmer for 5-6 minutes. Lightly toast pine nuts in a Teflon skillet. Add corn and heat through.

Add the corn and pine nuts to spinach and chives in a large bowl. Add crumbled bacon. Pour hot dressing over the mixture of spinach, chives, corn, pine nuts and bacon. Toss until leaves are well covered with dressing. Serve at once.

Spinach, Strawberry, Orange Salad
Serves 4

4 cups spinach, washed and chopped

1 cup strawberries, washed and sliced

1 can mandarin oranges, drained and chopped

1/4 cup currant or raspberry jelly

3 Tbs. raspberry or wine vinegar

1 tsp. fresh rosemary **or** 1/4 tsp. dried

Mix spinach, strawberries and oranges. Combine jelly and vinegar and heat until jelly dissolves. Stir in rosemary. Cool and pour over spinach and fruit. Toss lightly and serve.

HIGH COUNTRY HERBS

Macaroni Salad
Serves 6
This is another old standby that you can dress up or down
depending on what you have on hand.

1 cup macaroni, cooked

1 cup broccoli

1/2 red or green pepper, diced

1 small can sliced black olives

2 green onions
or
2 shallots, peeled and diced

2 tomatoes, diced

1 1/2 Tbs. olive oil

1 1/2 Tbs. wine vinegar

season salt and lemon pepper to taste

2 tsp. sugar

1 Tbs. chopped parsley

1/4 tsp. dried basil **or** 1 tsp. fresh basil, chopped

1 clove garlic, minced

Mix all together and chill to let flavors blend.

This is a very flexible salad. You can add some cooked diced chicken or ham. Instead of the vinegar and oil you might use mayonnaise. You might use cauliflower instead of broccoli or avacado or cucumber. Try adding chopped hard boiled eggs. Use what you have on hand, use your imagination, use whatever you like to eat and what sounds good!

Cucumber Garbanzo Bean Salad
Serves 8
This is another good delicious and nutritious salad

1 can garbanzo beans, drained

1 medium cucumber, sliced and quartered

1/2 cup sliced ripe olives

1/3 cup chopped red onion

1/4 cup minced fresh parsley

3 Tbs. vegetable oil

3 Tbs. red wine vinegar

1 Tbs. sugar

1 Tbs. fresh lemon juice

2 garlic cloves, minced

1/2 tsp. grated lemon peel

1/4 tsp. salt

1/8 tsp. pepper

Mix together first 5 ingredients. Mix together next 8 ingredients and pour over bean mixture. Chill and serve.

Raspberry Yogurt Vinaigrette
Makes 1 cup

1/2 cup plain yogurt

2 Tbs. raspberry vinegar

1 Tbs. mayonnaise

1 Tbs. honey or sugar

1 tsp. fresh rosemary, finely chopped

1/2 cup fresh or frozen raspberries (optional)

Mix the first 5 ingredients together with a whisk. Add raspberries if desired. Refrigerate until ready to use. This is a very low calorie, nearly fat free dressing. It is especially good on fruit salads or salads that combine lettuce and fruit.

HIGH COUNTRY HERBS

Cajun Potato Salad
Serves 6
A very different but delicious variation on another old standby!

2 lbs. small red potatoes

1/2 cup red onion, chopped

1/2 cup green onions, sliced

1/4 cup fresh parsley, minced

6 Tbs. cider vinegar

1/2 lb. precooked kielbasa or Cajun sausage, sliced

6 Tbs. olive oil

1 Tbs. Dijon mustard

2 cloves garlic, minced

1/2 tsp. pepper

1/4 to 1/2 tsp. cayenne pepper (optional)

Cook potatoes until tender and drain. Cool and cut into 1/4 inch slices. Place in a large bowl and add onions, 3 Tbs. vinegar, and parsley and toss. Cook sausage in oil until it just begins to brown. Remove and add to potato mixture. To drippings add mustard, garlic, pepper, cayenne (if desired), and remaining vinegar. Bring to a boil and pour over potato mixture. Serve at once.

Honey Mustard Salad Dressing
Makes 1 cup
This is one of my favorite salad dressings. It is very low calorie.

1/2 cup plain yogurt

3 Tbs. mayonnaise

3 Tbs. honey

2 Tbs. Dijon mustard

1 Tbs. prepared mustard

2 1/2 tsp. white wine vinegar

Mix all together with a whisk.

Refrigerate until ready to use.

HIGH COUNTRY HERBS

The Vegetables

HIGH COUNTRY HERBS

Vegetables

I read somewhere that if you eat vegetables for a hundred years, you won't die young.

I love vegetables. I can make a meal of vegetables very easily. I have, on occasion been accused of being a vegetarian and I guess that is quite close to the truth. Although I am not a full- fledged vegetarian, it doesn't bother me at all to go without meat.

Last year I raised some blue potatoes. I dug one fresh from the ground, washed it and baked it, cut it open, mashed it with a fork and covered it with sour cream and freshly chopped chives. Now if this was not the ambrosia, it is about the closest I have ever come.

I come close to worshiping tomatoes, peppers and eggplant. I can and do eat broccoli, cauliflower and Brussel sprouts several times a week. Green beans, peas and corn bring me to ecstasy. Then there are sweet potatoes, yams, winter squash, summer squash, pumpkin, cucumbers, greens of all sorts, and on and on. And mind you, I grow them all myself. I spend hours in January poring through seed catalogues, reading about the virtues of all the varieties of each of the different vegetables, wishing I had room to grow more, wanting to try one of every kind, changing my mind a dozen times before placing my order.

When the seeds finally arrive, I set up my planting trays, fill them with soil-less mix, add each seed and the appropriate label. Then I wait impatiently for the seeds to sprout. I tend them carefully, until I can transfer them to the garden, where I await my first harvest with joy and expectation. Once you gather a bunch of fresh lettuces and spinach, add some chopped fresh herbs, and sprinkle on your homemade dressing, it's hard to go back to produce and dressings you buy from the grocery store.

The amazing flavor of a homegrown tomato has to mean it is full of vitamins and minerals and other things that are good for you, unlike the hard flavorless, round red things the grocers offer you. There is no comparison in flavor and goodness between what you grow yourself and vegetables that are shipped in and may have been picked months before you buy them. The addition of homegrown herbs merely enhances the already great taste of homegrown vegetables.

Here are a few of my favorite recipes.

Garlic Mashed Potatoes
Serves 4-6

Peel and quarter five to six medium potatoes, (I prefer Yukon Gold) and place in a large pan, with 4 to 6 cloves of garlic, peeled. Add enough water to almost cover the potatoes, cover the pan, and bring to a boil.

Turn the heat to medium and cook until the potatoes are tender when pierced with a fork. Drain and mash with chicken broth or milk that has been warmed. (I like to use a ricer to mash my potatoes, and then stir in about 1 Tbs. of butter and enough warmed chicken broth to make a nice consistency.)

Add about 1/4 cup of chopped fresh parsley or chives, if you like. Stir well. Pour into a bowl. Place a nice pat of butter on top and garnish with a little more herb. Serve immediately.

Variations

Another way to fix mashed potatoes is to peel and dice an onion. Heat 2 Tbs. of olive oil in a skillet and add the onion. Cook until it is lightly browned and limp. Stir into the mashed potatoes. Then add in a tablespoon or two of grated horseradish. Mound into a dish, put a pat of butter in a well on top, and sprinkle with chopped parsley, chives, or chervil.

If you have leftover mashed potatoes, you can stir in one cup of grated cheese to three cups of potatoes and add 2 beaten eggs, and whatever herb, onion, or garlic you like. Pour it into a greased oven proof dish. Bake at 350 degrees until it is heated through and puffed, about 30 to 40 minutes.

Or you can make potato patties or pancakes out of leftover mashed potatoes. To one cup cf mashed potatoes add 1 beaten egg, 1/4 cup flour and a little milk. Add onion flakes and parsley, if you don't already have flavorings in the potatoes. Heat 2 Tbs. olive oil in a skillet, form the potatoes into patties and fry until golden brown. Turn and brown the other side. Serve hot. Swedish potato pancakes generally are made with plain mashed potatoes the same as above. But instead of other seasonings, add 1/2 tsp. of nutmeg.

Stuffed Mushrooms with Garlic
Serves 4
(unless I get selfish and eat it all myself!)

While mushrooms are not vegetables, they are often served in place of a vegetable. And they are so good, they deserve a place in the book, so here they are.

Start with about a dozen large Italian brown, or white, mushrooms. Pull the stems loose and gently wash the caps and set aside to drain. Wash the stems and chop them finely.

Heat 2 Tbs. of olive oil in a skillet. Stir in one peeled and chopped shallot and 2 to 3 cloves of garlic, crushed. When the shallot and garlic are golden brown, stir in the mushroom stems and cook for a few minutes. Add 1/2 cup bread crumbs, 1/2 cup grated Parmesan or Asiago cheese, 2 Tbs. chopped parsley and 2 Tbs. chopped chives. Add salt and pepper to taste. Mix well and remove from the heat.

Lightly oil a flat baking dish. Fill each mushroom cap with the mixture and set it into the baking dish. Bake at 350 degrees for 30 minutes. Put caps on serving dish, drizzle with juices from the bottom of the baking dish and sprinkle with Parmesan and parsley. Serve at once.

HIGH COUNTRY HERBS

Oven Roasted Vegetables

Spray or lightly oil a baking sheet. Cut small red potatoes in half. Slice eggplant and zucchini into 1/2 inch thick slices. Peel small scallions, cutting back the tops, leaving about 1 inch of green. Wash asparagus and remove the lower, woody portion of the stem. Peel and slice onions into 1/2 inch wedges. Peel, seed and slice bell peppers into 1/2 inch slices. Remove stems from the mushrooms.

You may also use beets, peeled and quartered, peeled and sliced yams, slices of summer squash, peeled and sliced winter squash, or Roma tomatoes, sliced in half with seeds removed.

Once you have your tray of vegetables ready, mix 2 cloves of garlic (minced or crushed) with 3 to 4 Tbs. of olive oil and 2 Tbs. of your favorite herb, chopped. (You might use basil, rosemary, oregano, tarragon, parsley or chives, or a combination.) Drizzle the olive oil - herb mixture over the veggies and bake at 375 degrees for 30 to 45 minutes. Serve hot.

Oven roasted vegetables of your choice are so flavorful you'll wonder why you ever fixed them any other way. They can make a meal simply by adding a good hardy bread. Or serve them with pasta tossed with garlic and olive oil, or butter, garlic and parsley. Or as a side dish with baked chicken or grilled pork chops. Any way you serve them, they will get rave reviews.

HIGH COUNTRY HERBS

Slow Roasted Tomatoes

These are infinitely better than commercially dried
tomatoes with so much more flavor.
I make them a cookie sheet full at a time.

Preheat oven to 300 degrees.

Wash Roma tomatoes and slice in half lengthwise. With a spoon, remove the seeds. Place on lightly oiled baking sheet. Lightly spray the tomatoes with olive oil, then sprinkle with a mixture of sea salt and freshly ground pepper, garlic powder and chopped parsley, thyme, oregano, basil, or marjoram, or a mixture of all. Use about 1 tsp. dried or 1 Tbs. fresh herbs.

Bake uncovered for about 2 hours. If they look too dry after 1 hour, spray with a little more oil. These are great served with some cheese and a nice crusty peasant type bread. Dice them on top of pasta or salad. Put them on a pizza with pesto and artichokes and just a sprinkling of cheese.

You can store unused roasted tomatoes in the refrigerator or freeze them for later use. I like to freeze things like this laid out individually on a cookie sheet and then put them in a freezer bag so that I don't have one big lump of frozen stuff.

After you try these, you will want to keep a supply on hand.

HIGH COUNTRY HERBS

Baked Tomatoes with Peppers and Herbs
Serves 4

This is another dish I am happy to comsume all by myself though I am sometimes willing to share it with a VERY good friend!

4-6 large bell peppers (red or yellow)

Roast peppers until the skin is blackened, then place in a bowl and cover the bowl with a plate. Let the peppers steam until cool enough to handle, then remove the peelings, seed them, and cut them into strips. While the peppers are cooling, take about 6 tomatoes – a combination of red and yellow is good – and dip them in boiling water until the skins loosen. Peel them, gently squeeze out the seeds if desired and cut into large chunks.

Mix together:

1 tsp. minced garlic

2 Tbs. chopped fresh parsley

2 Tbs. capers

1 Tbs. fresh marjoram or basil, chopped

3 Tbs. olive oil

Salt and pepper to taste

Place peppers and tomatoes in a large ovenproof pie pan. Cover with foil and bake at 400 degrees for about 20 minutes. Cool slightly and serve. Sprinkle with grated Parmesan or Romano cheese, if desired. This makes a good side dish with most meats and a good crusty bread.

Moo Shu Vegetables
Serves 4
These are a good, quick low calorie lunch.
Much better for you than a double bacon cheeseburger
and an order of fries.

6 Chinese dried mushrooms
   cover with boiling water and let sit for 20 minutes.

2 Tbs. olive oil

2 cloves garlic, minced

1 tsp. grated fresh ginger root

2 Tbs. flat leaf parsley, chopped

2 cups shredded cabbage

1 red bell pepper, diced

1 cup bean sprouts

2 large green onions

1 Tbs. hoisin sauce

3 Tbs. plum sauce

Tortillas

Slice the mushrooms after they are reconstituted. Heat the olive oil in a heavy skillet or wok. Stir fry mushrooms, garlic, and ginger for one minute, or until garlic is golden. Add cabbage and red pepper. Stir fry for 3 minutes more. Add bean sprouts and onions and stir fry 2 minutes more. Stir in sauces and parsley and heat through. Serve on tortillas.

Antipasto Bowl
Serves 12
This is a wonderful dish for a buffet supper.

3 cups of asparagus,
> woody bottoms removed, washed and broken into 2 inch pieces. Steam these for about 2 1/2 minutes.

3 cups mushrooms
> Remove stems and set aside for another use.
> Slice mushrooms into 1/4 inch slices.

1 cup of red bell peppers, seeded and cut into strips

1/2 cup pitted black olives (I like to use Greek)

3 ounces cubed mozzarella cheese

1 - 14 ounce can of artichoke hearts drained and cut
> into chunks

1 - 11 ounce jar pepperocini peppers, drained

Place all vegetables in a large bowl

Mix together:

1/3 cup white wine vinegar

2 Tbs. olive oil

2 tsp. dried basil
or
oregano
or
a combination
or
1 Tbs. fresh, chopped

2 Tbs. fresh parsley, chopped **or** 3 tsp. dried

1 Tbs. sugar

3 cloves garlic, crushed

Freshly ground pepper to taste

Pour over vegetables. Cover and refrigerate for several hours or overnight. Remove from refrigerator and allow to come almost to room temperature before serving. Delicious with a pasta dinner. Be sure to include some really good homemade bread.

The Meats,
Poultry & Fish

HIGH COUNTRY HERBS

The Meats, Poultry & Fish

There are many different meats and many different ways of preparing them. In this region, many people depend on wild game meat and fish as their primary source of protein. I have heard many people say they don't care for the flavor of wild game, and just as many people who love the taste. Regardless of which category you fall into, herbs will enhance the flavor of almost any meat, poultry or fish, without the addition of the preservatives, MSG, sodium nitrite, and quantities of salt found in prepared meats.

I have already given you the recipe for Turkey Baste. (see Seasonings) Although this is called "Turkey" Baste, it is equally good on pheasant, quail or chicken. You can use it as a marinade if you are going to grill the meat. Or you can use it as a baste, meaning to pour it over the bird, and inside the bird before baking. It makes the meat tender, moist and flavorful, without any additional salt or other seasoning. If you feel the need of other seasoning, sprinkle on some lightly crushed rosemary, or use the Poultry Seasoning recipe from the Seasonings section of this book.

For beef, pork, elk, deer or antelope you can use any of the seasonings or Rubs from the Seasonings section or some of the recipes that follow. A "Rub" is simply what it sounds like: You sprinkle the seasoning on the meat and rub it in. Do this to both sides. I like to let it set for about a half an hour to absorb the flavors after rubbing the seasoning into the meat. Then you can grill it or bake it or sauté it, whatever you had in mind.

Herbed Pork Roast
Serves 4-6
The next time you are cooking a pork roast, try this recipe.

3 Tbs. parsley, finely chopped

2 tsp. paprika

2 tsp. dried basil

2 tsp. sea salt (optional)

1 tsp. pepper

1 tsp. garlic powder

1 tsp. dried oregano

1/2 tsp crushed fennel seed

1/2 tsp. dried thyme

Mix together seasonings and rub into a 2 pound pork roast. I like to use pork tenderloin as it is very low in fat.

Bake uncovered in a shallow roasting pan at 325 degrees for 35 minutes per pound or until internal temperature reaches 160 -170 degrees. Let rest for ten minutes after removing from the oven and slice into 1/2 inch thick slices.

I might say here that I use sea salt because it has a much lower percentage of sodium and also trace minerals, which we all need. It also does not contain the sugar that is found in regular table salt. (Yes, really. Read the label !) If you are going to use salt in your cooking, why not use a healthier version?

Sweet & Sour Pork
Serves 4-6

1 can pineapple chunks

1 1/4 lb. pork tenderloin

1/3 cup pineapple juice

2 Tbs. soy sauce

1 clove garlic, minced

2 tsp. brown sugar

2 Tbs. cornstarch

1 Tbs. vegetable oil

2 tsp. ginger root, minced

8 green onions cut into 1 inch pieces

1 red bell pepper, seeded and diced

1/4 cup catsup

1/3 cup chicken broth

Mix pineapple juice, soy sauce, garlic, ginger, brown sugar, cornstarch, catsup, and chicken broth in a bowl. Cut pork into 1 inch cubes and place in bowl with marinade. Let stand 30 to 60 minutes.

Remove meat with a slotted spoon. Heat oil in Teflon skillet or wok and add meat. Cook and stir over high heat until meat browns. Add green onion and red pepper and stir fry 2 to 3 minutes. Add marinade and cook until thick and clear. Stir in pineapple. Serve over rice, rice noodles or Chinese noodles.

David's Green Chili
(My son David's favorite!)
Serves 6-8

1 lb. pork chops, bones and fat removed,
    cut into small cubes

1 lb. lean hamburger

1 onion, chopped

2 cloves garlic, crushed

3 to 4 cans diced green chilies
or
7 - 8 Anaheim chilies, seeded and diced.
    For more heat, you can also add two or three Jalapeños.

   If you prefer the chilies peeled, put them under your broiler, or hold them on a fork over a gas flame until they are blackened and the skin is blistered. Place in a large bowl and cover with a plate. Let sit until cool enough to handle. The skins should come off easily. Then seed and dice.

1/2 cup chicken broth

1 Tbs. flour

1 tsp. chili powder

1 tsp. cumin

1 Tbs. parsley, finely chopped

1 tsp. oregano, finely chopped
(the Mexican oregano is best if you can find it)

salt and pepper to taste

Brown the meat well. Add onion and garlic. Cook until the onion is clear. Add green chilies and chicken broth. Stir until slightly thickened. Serve with tortilla chips and cheese, or on tortillas.

This can also be used to make great quesadillas:

Quesadillas

Lay out a tortilla, place about 2 large tablespoons of green chili on one half of the tortilla, and cover with shredded Monterey Jack cheese, or other cheese of your choice.

Fold the tortilla in half, over the meat and cheese. Bake on a hot griddle or skillet that has been lightly covered with oil. Cook until lightly browned, then carefully turn and brown the other side.

Serve with refried beans and salsa. Add a little sour cream and chopped Chives or Cilantro, if you wish.

Spiced Pork Chops
Serves 4

4 boneless loin chops

1/2 cup flour

1 1/2 tsp. garlic powder

1 1/2 tsp. ground mustard

1 1/2 tsp. paprika

1/2 tsp. celery salt

1/4 tsp. ground ginger

1/8 tsp. dried oregano

1/8 tsp. dried basil

1/8 tsp. salt

1/8 tsp. pepper

4 pork loin chops

1 to 2 tsp. cooking oil

1 cup ketchup

1 cup water

1/4 cup packed brown sugar

In a shallow dish combine the first ten ingredients. Roll pork chops in flour mixture. In a skillet, brown pork chops in oil on both sides.

Place in greased 9 x 13 inch baking dish. Combine ketchup, water, and brown sugar. Pour over chops. Bake uncovered at 350 degrees for one hour.

Any time you prefer to use fresh herbs, please do so. Use them at about twice the amount of dried herb. For instance, in this recipe, you would use 1/4 tsp. finely minced basil instead of the 1/8 tsp. dried.

Beef Tenderloin
or
Prime Rib Roast
Serves 6

1 tsp. dried oregano

1 tsp. paprika

1 tsp. thyme

1 tsp. sea salt

1 tsp. garlic powder

1 tsp. onion powder

1/2 tsp. freshly ground pepper

1/2 tsp. white pepper

1/4 tsp. cayenne pepper

1 beef roast, approximately 3 pounds

Mix the seasoning and rub them into the roast. Place the roast on a rack in a roasting pan and bake at 425 degrees, uncovered until the meat is cooked as you like it. Allow 45 to 50 minutes per pound for rare, 55 to 60 minutes for medium rare, 60 to 65 for medium and 65 to 70 for well done. The best way to tell the doneness of beef roast is with a meat thermometer.

When the meat is done the way you like it, remove it from the pan to a platter. Allow it to rest for 10 minutes before slicing it into half inch thick slices.

Mix up some horseradish sauce to serve on the side.

Horseradish Sauce

Mix equal parts horseradish and mayonnaise and add some chives if you like.

Barbequed Beef Roast
Serves 6

1 3/4 cup chili sauce

2 Tbs. tomato paste

1/4 cup maple syrup **or** molasses

2 Tbs. light corn syrup

2 Tbs. wine vinegar

1 Tbs. light soy sauce

1 1/2 tsp. olive oil

2 cloves garlic, minced

1 onion, chopped

1 Tbs. fresh parsley, chopped

2 lb. beef roast rubbed well with Barbeque Rub **or**
Indian Masala

Mix together first 6 ingredients. Heat olive oil in Dutch oven. Add onions, garlic and parsley, and cook until clear and light golden brown. Move the onion and garlic to one side and brown roast well on both sides. Cover with sauce made from the first 6 ingredients.

Bake covered at 350 degrees for about 2 hours or until tender. Remove meat and keep warm. Reduce sauce until desired consistency is reached. Slice roast and serve sauce on the side.

Leftovers may be sliced and heated in the sauce and served on a hearty bun for delicious sandwiches.

Turkey Fajitas
Serves 6
This is a very low fat recipe.

1 lb. boneless turkey breast

1 green bell pepper cut into strips or diced

1 red bell pepper cut into strips or diced

1 red **or** white onion, diced

1/3 cup chili sauce

3 Tbs. lime juice

1/4 tsp. cayenne pepper

2 cloves garlic, crushed

1/2 tsp. ginger root, minced

1 Tbs. parsley, chopped

1 tsp. oregano, minced

1 Tbs. olive oil

Flour tortillas

Combine chili sauce, lime juice and spices. Set aside.

Heat oil in Teflon skillet or wok. Cut turkey into strips and stir fry until turkey is lightly browned. Add onion and cook until limp. Stir in pepper strips and cook for 3 minutes, stirring constantly. Add chili sauce mixture and cook 2 or 3 minutes longer or until turkey is done. Heat flour tortillas. Serve with lettuce, sour cream, guacamole, salsa, hot peppers, and/or diced tomatoes as desired.

Curried Chicken
Serves 4
Try this for something different. You might like it!

1 - 3 1/2 lb. chicken quartered, skin removed

1/4 cup butter, divided

3 cloves garlic, minced

2 cups yellow onion, diced

1 carrot, diced

1 stalk celery, diced

1 green apple, cored and diced (optional)

2-3 Tbs. curry powder

1 Tbs. paprika

2 dried chili peppers, crushed (optional)

1 cup tomato juice

1 cup chicken stock

1 - 2 Tbs. cornstarch dissolved in 1/4 cup cold water

Melt 2 Tbs. butter in a heavy skillet with a lid or a Dutch oven. Quickly brown the chicken, then cover the pan and place in the oven. Bake at 350 degrees of 15 minutes a pound, or until chicken is done.

Remove meat from chicken, cool, remove the bones and dice. While chicken is cooling, sauté the vegetables and apple in 2 Tbs. butter until onion is transparent. Stir in seasonings. Add chicken, tomato juice, and stock. Cover and simmer over low heat until vegetables are cooked, about 30 minutes.

Stir in cornstarch. Cook until thickened. Serve over rice.

Crispy Baked Chicken

1/4 cup cornmeal (the more finely ground, the better)

1/4 cup flour

1/2 cup flour

1 1/2 tsp. salt

1 1/2 tsp. chili powder

1/2 tsp. oregano

1/4 tsp. pepper

1 fryer chicken 3 to 3 1/2 lbs., cut up

1/2 cup milk

1/3 cup olive oil, **or** butter

Combine first six ingredients. Dip chicken in milk and roll in cornmeal/flour mixture until the pieces are well coated. Place the pieces in well oiled 9 x 13 inch baking dish. Drizzle with butter or spray with olive oil. Bake uncovered at 375 degrees for 50 to 55 minutes.

HIGH COUNTRY HERBS

Broiled or Grilled Fish

4 Tbs. light soy sauce or Wasabi

2 Tbs. lemon juice

1 tsp. olive oil

1 clove garlic, minced

1/4 tsp. tarragon, dill, or basil, minced

1 Tbs. parsley, minced

Mix all together and brush on fish steaks or fillets several times. Sprinkle with lemon pepper. Broil or grill as desired.

HIGH COUNTRY HERBS

Your Just Desserts

HIGH COUNTRY HERBS

Your Just Desserts

Very few desserts have herbs in them, other than mints and spices. But after all your hard work, why not take a cup or glass of herb tea out to your garden, along with one of the following delights, sit back, relax and enjoy what you have created, if for only a little while. You deserve it.

Most of these recipes are also wonderful to include in a gift basket so they really do belong here!

And of course, since few among us can resist chocolate, let's start with brownies.

HIGH COUNTRY HERBS

Brownies
Makes 9

Melt together one stick of butter and 2 squares of unsweetened chocolate.

Stir in 1 cup of sugar, 2 eggs and 1/2 tsp. vanilla. Beat well. (You may also add a tsp. of cinnamon if you like.)

Add 1/4 cup flour and 1 cup chopped nuts (walnuts, pecans or hazelnuts are all good additions, or leave them out if you don't like nuts. Or add 1/2 cup white chocolate chips and 1/2 cup dark chocolate chips as another option.)

Butter and flour an 8 inch square baking pan. Pour in the brownie mixture and spread evenly. Bake at 325 degrees for about 40 minutes. Watch carefully so they don't get too well done.

Cut into squares and stack on a platter.

For something really delicious, put a brownie on a plate, mound on some whipped cream, garnish with chopped mint leaves and a few raspberries.

HIGH COUNTRY HERBS

Lemon Bars
Makes 9
This is a favorite dessert after a heavy meal
or in the summer when it is too hot to eat.

1/3 cup butter

2 tsp. grated lemon peel

1 cup sugar

3 Tbs. lemon juice (juice of one lemon)

1 cup flour

2 eggs

2 Tbs. flour

1/4 tsp. baking powder

Beat butter until creamy. Add 1/4 cup sugar and beat until well mixed. Stir in 1 cup flour until crumbly. Press into the bottom of an 8 inch square pan and bake at 350 degrees for 15 minutes.

Combine the rest of the ingredients and beat until thoroughly combined. Pour over crust and bake at 350 degrees for 20 minutes or until the filling is set. Sprinkle with powdered sugar. Cut into squares and serve.

HIGH COUNTRY HERBS

Janie's Best Ever Chocolate Chip Cookies
Makes about 3 Dozen

2/3 cup shortening

2/3 cup butter

1 cup brown sugar

1 cup white sugar

1 tsp. vanilla

2 large eggs

3 cups flour

1 tsp. baking powder

1 tsp. baking soda

1/2 tsp. cinnamon

12 oz. chocolate chips

1 cup chopped pecans

Cream together shortening, butter, and sugars. Stir in eggs and vanilla. Add flour, baking powder and baking soda. Stir in chocolate chips and pecans. Drop by rounded teaspoons on an ungreased cookie sheet. Bake at 350 degrees for 10 to 12 minutes.

My daughter, Janie, mixes up various kinds of cookie dough, puts the dough in covered plastic buckets and gives them as gifts along with the recipe. She keeps the mixed dough in the freezer until she is ready to give it.

Add some spiced tea mix, hot chocolate or cappuccino mix in a basket for a great gift.

Mitch's Peanut Butter Balls
Makes about 100

These taste like Reese's Peanut Butter Cups. They are delicious. My son, Mitch, makes these every Christmas to include in his Christmas baskets. He always receives rave reviews and requests for more.

1 stick butter, melted

1/2 tsp. vanilla

18 ounce jar chunky peanut butter

1 lb. box powdered sugar

5 cups Rice Krispies

1/2 cup chopped peanuts (optional)

Mix butter, peanut butter and vanilla together well. Then stir in powdered sugar, Rice Krispies, and nuts. Mix well. Roll into balls the size of a walnut.

Place in freezer until cold. Dip in either white chocolate almond bark, or semi-sweet chocolate. Set on waxed paper to harden. You can always freeze them and dip them later, too.

HIGH COUNTRY HERBS

Triple Chocolate Zucchini Muffins
Makes 12 Muffins
These are so good you'll never give away your zucchini again!

2 eggs

1 3/4 cups sugar

1 cup buttermilk

1/2 cup oil

1 tsp. vanilla

4 Tbs. cocoa

1/2 tsp. baking powder

1 tsp. baking soda

2 1/2 cups flour

1 tsp. cinnamon

1 pkg. instant vanilla pudding

2 cups grated zucchini

1/2 cup chocolate chips

1/2 cup white chocolate chips
1/2 to 1 cup nuts (optional)

Cream together the first five ingredients. Sift together the next five ingredients and add to creamed mixture. Add pudding and zucchini and mix well. Stir in chocolate chips and nuts. Bake in large muffin tins or 9 by 13 cake pan that has been greased and floured.

Bake at 325 degrees 40 to 45 minutes or until toothpick comes out clean.

Dried Fruit Cake
Makes 5 Small Loaves

Okay, I hear you. "I hate fruitcake!" you say. Well this fruitcake is so far from that single fruitcake that has been passed around the world for the last 50 years, it is unbelievable. It is simply delicious and makes a great addition to Christmas baskets

2 cups sugar

2 cups water

1 cup brandy

2 cups chopped pitted dates

2 cups golden raisins

2 cups dried sweet cherries

1 1/2 cups dried apricots, diced

1 cup dried cranberries

1/2 cup butter

Mix together and bring to a boil. Simmer for 10 minutes. Allow to cool completely.

2 cups flour

HIGH COUNTRY HERBS

2 cups sliced almonds

1 tsp. cinnamon

1/2 tsp. nutmeg

1/2 tsp. salt

1/2 tsp. baking soda

2 large eggs

1 Tbs. almond extract

Mix all together with first ingredients. Pour in greased floured pans. Bake at 300 degrees for 1 hour and 15 minutes or until done.

I bake these in small loaf pans. The recipe makes 5 of these small cakes. After the cakes are cool, remove from the pans, wrap in colored Saran Wrap or aluminum foil, add a bow, and put them in a basket with some really good tea, scone mix and a jar of jam. Anyone would be pleased with such a grand gift.

HIGH COUNTRY HERBS

Gifts from
Your Garden

HIGH COUNTRY HERBS

The Gifts

Throughout the first part of this book I have offered ideas for gift baskets as well as mix packets and seasonings. Food is the ideal gift. It is always welcome. You don't have to find a place to keep it, as it is soon used up. It is usually less expensive than buying something from the store. And above all, homemade gifts show that you care enough to be thoughtful in choosing a gift, that you are willing to spend your time to create something special.

Even if you don't wish to make everything or, for that matter anything in a gift basket, it can still be unique and long remembered because you put together items that you choose especially for the recipient into a decorative and attractive presentation. And don't forget that something as simple as a shaker of season salt or a baguette of homemade bread makes a wonderful hostess gift when visiting friends.

HIGH COUNTRY HERBS

Gift Basket Ideas:

Gardener's Basket

If you have a friend who loves to garden, and I'll bet you do,
try putting together something like this:

Some gardener's soap or hand cream

A new garden trowel or a nice pair of clippers

A pair of gloves

Several packages of seed

A soil thermometer or a pH tester

An herbal Bath Bag or a soothing Bath Brew

A good insect repellant.
> (With West Nile Virus becoming such a threat, this could
> be quite welcome!)

You can make the basket as simple or elaborate as you
wish. A few packets of garden seeds tied with a nice bow in a small
basket can be a great gift. Or you can fill a large basket or tool
carrier with all sorts of things for gardening like those mentioned
above. Let your imagination and creativity run rampant. The fun
is in giving a gift especially chosen for your recipient.

HIGH COUNTRY HERBS

Soothing Bath Brew
This also makes a great gift for your gardener friends!

2 cups rosemary (relieves stiff joints)

1 cup bay leaves (relieves aches and pains)

1 1/2 cups sage leaves (aids joints and muscles)

1 cup lavender flowers and leaves
   (fragrance and relaxation)

1 cup calendula flower petals
   (soothes the skin and adds a nice color)

Mix together and store in a covered container

Cover half cup herbs with boiling water and let steep for half an hour. Pour liquid into bath water. Light a lavender candle. Put on some soothing music. Lean back, relax and let this delightful concoction soak away tired, aching joints and muscles.

Or you could make a Bath Bag like this:

Sew together two six inch squares of terry cloth, leaving a small opening in one corner, or fold a washcloth in half and sew the same way. Mix one cup of oatmeal with one cup of herbs, like those in the previous recipe. Fill the bag until nicely stuffed. Sew the opening shut. Throw the bag into the bath under the faucet. Leave as the tub fills. Rub the bag over the body to soothe wind burned skin and achy joints. When done with your bath, wring out the bag and hang to dry. It can generally be reused several times.

HIGH COUNTRY HERBS

Black & Red Chili Mix to Go
Serves 8

2 Tbs. dried onion

1 Tbs. chili powder

2 tsp. ground cumin

2 tsp. oregano

2 tsp. cocoa

1 tsp. crushed red pepper flakes

1 bay leaf

1/2 cup sun dried tomatoes, diced

Mix all together and place in a small plastic bag.

1 cup dried kidney beans

2 cups dried black beans

In 1 quart jar layer 1 cup black beans, then 1 cup kidney beans, then 1 cup black beans, and place the bag of spices on top. Screw on lid. Decorate as desired and include the cooking instructions:

To make the chili, cover beans with water and bring to a

boil. Let sit for 1 hour.

In the meantime, brown 2 pounds of beef, or 1 pound of pork and 1 pound of beef, either ground or diced. Add spices. Stir in 3 cans of beef or chicken broth or 6 cups water. Drain beans and add to meat and spices. Cook until beans are done, 2-3 hours or more. (May add 1 1/2 cups frozen corn when beans are done, if you like, or a can of tomato sauce or diced tomatoes.) Cook for 5 more minutes, or until heated through.

Serve with sour cream or grated cheese if desired. Or Indian Fry Bread or Corn Bread, or crackers.

Some Other Ideas

Think about who you want to give a gift to. Perhaps an elderly neighbor who enjoys reading. Make a pint of soup, add a small loaf of bread, a brownie or two, a couple of tea bags or some instant coffee, and a good book.

If you have a friend who likes to grill outside in the summer, make up a basket of meat seasonings like Turkey Baste, Poultry Seasoning, Barbeque Rub, Meat Seasoning and Indian Masala along with instructions for use. Add the Seasoning Salt and Lemon Pepper to make a larger basket. Or simply give the Seasoning Salt and Lemon Pepper in a small basket.

You can make a simple Bread and Cheese Basket, or enlarge it with a small jar a Baba Ghanoush and a quart of homemade soup.

For a wedding gift, two friends and myself went together and made a large Italian basket. We lined a large basket with two nice cloth napkins, added a bottle of Italian seasoning, a baguette of bread, a wedge of Parmesan cheese and a cheese grater, a bottle of wine and a corkscrew, a jar of minced garlic, some homemade pasta, a jar of basil pesto, an Italian cookbook, and a small box of imported chocolates. This was a very big hit with the new bride and groom.

You could make a Mexican Basket with Chili Powder, Indian Fry Bread Mix, or Cornbread Mix and Red and Black Chili Mix.

You can make an English Tea Basket or a French Basket. Look up some ideas for a Scandinavian, German or Russian basket. Make a Chinese basket with the Stir Fry Seasoning, a jar of Preserved Ginger and another of the Plum sauce. Add a bottle of hot mustard, some rice or rice noodles and a good Chinese cookbook.

· Make your gifts personal. Make the gift fit the person you are giving them to. Gift baskets are only limited by your imagination and creativity. I hope you get as much enjoyment out of giving gifts like these as I do; as much pleasure as the recipients seem to derive from such thoughtfulness.

HIGH COUNTRY HERBS

Sources

HIGH COUNTRY HERBS

The Sources

These are a few of the sources available to you. I am sure you also have your own favorite companies. And of course, your bestsources are your local nurseries and health food stores. As for other books on the subject, I am sure you can find many good books on cooking, gardening, and herbs at your local library. Look them over and see which ones you like, which ones you might like to own. Some of my favorites are:

Any of the Rodale Press gardening books.
A great resource with lots of clear illustrations

The Perfect Mix by Diane Phillips
Many examples of gift mixes.

Eight Weeks to Optimum Health by Dr. Andrew Weil
and
Eating Well for Optimum Health by Dr. Andrew Weil
Inspirations for good food and good health.

The Sunset Western Garden Book
Quite simply the best overall reference for growing anything in this region.

Here are some good sources for seeds and plants that you can't find locally:

Burgess Seed and Plant Company 1-309-663-9551
or **www.eBurgess.com**

The Cook's Garden 1-800-457-9703
or **www.cooksgarden.com**
Many different kinds of seeds. Some that are hard to find and unusual.

Frontier Natural Products 1-800-786-1388
A great source of bulk herbs and spices, as well as organic products and natural remedies.

Gardens Alive 1-513-354-1483
or **www.GardensAlive.com**
Good products to help you grow your best garden ever.

Gardener's Supply Company 1-800-427-3363
or **www.gardeners.com**
Many different products for the garden.

Jung's Quality Seed 1-800-247-5864
or **www.jungseed.com**
A good selection of seeds.

Park's Seeds 1-800-845-3369

or **www.parkseed.com**

A good seed company.

Pinetree Garden Seeds 1-207-926-3400
or **www.superseeds.com**

A wide selection of seeds to choose from.

Renee's Garden (part of Shepard's Seeds)
www.reneesgarden.com

A good source of unusual varieties.

R.H. Shumway 1-800-342-9461
or **www.rhschumway.com**

Plants and seeds with many heirlooms.

Richters Herbs
or **www.richters.com**

Many unusual herb plants. A good source

Seeds of Change 1-888-762-7333
or **www.seedsofchange.com**

A good choice for organic seeds and products.

Shepard's Garden Seeds
(a division of White Flower Farms)
1-800-503 9624
or **www.whiteflowerfarm.com**

A good source of unusual imported varieties and unusual things for your garden.

Territorial Seed Company 1-541-942-9547
or www.territorialseed.com

A good source of organic seeds and plants.

Totally Tomatoes 1-800-345-5977

or www.totallytomato.com

If you can't find the tomato you are looking for in this catalogue, maybe you are being to picky.

HIGH COUNTRY HERBS

Index

Peppers

About the Author...

Cheryl Anderson Wright was born and raised in Boone, Iowa. At an early age her father taught her to garden and her Grandmother taught her to cook. These two things started a lifelong love of both.

In 1979, she moved to Cody, Wyoming with her husband and three children. There she feels she really began to learn the true meaning of gardening.

She has worked at many jobs over the years including several years at Wyoming Game and Fish and several for Wyoming State Parks and is currently employed at the Park County Library. She is a member of Audubon, Cody Writers, and the local garden club. Cheryl is enrolled at Colorado Community College Online seeking a degree in Library Science. As a Master Gardener-in-training, she spends a great deal of time perfecting her gardening skills and giving talks on raising and cooking with herbs.

She enjoys writing poetry and working on family history, as well as writing stories of her ancestors. She has had several pieces published in Woven on the Wind, the Hardground Anthologies, and Fence Post magazine. She won the Thorpe Award for poetry for a poem about her Grandmother.

HIGH COUNTRY HERBS

Printed in the United States
975000007B

9 780971 472587